THE
NAPOLEONIC SOLDIER

THE
NAPOLEONIC
SOLDIER

STEPHEN E. MAUGHAN

The Crowood Press

First published in 1999 by
The Crowood Press Ltd
Ramsbury, Marlborough
Wiltshire SN8 2HR

British Library Cataloguing-in-Publication Data
A catalogue record for this book is available
from the British Library

ISBN 1 86126 281 7

Edited by Martin Windrow
Designed by Frank Ainscough / Compendium
Printed and bound by Craft Print Pte Ltd

DEDICATION
This book is dedicated to the memory of my father
Edward Maughan, 1925-95,
who taught me to love history and horses.

ACKNOWLEDGEMENTS
The author wishes to record his gratitude to the many re-enactors whose patience and hard work made possible the photographic sessions which provided the illustrations in this book. Anyone interested in Napoleonic re-enactment can contact Mike Freeman of the Napoleonic Association at 5 Thingwall Drive, Irby, Wirral, Merseyside, L61 3XN.
Horses were kindly supplied by Corinne and Donald Dingly of Middleton Equestrian Centre; their help and advice was greatly appreciated. Other horses were provided by Janet Rogers, who specialises in historical equestrian events.
Angela Lowes has reconstructed several uniforms for the book.
Master saddler Alex Marsh has reconstructed saddles, bridles and soldier's belting, and Paul Scarrett-Jones worked on period bits and much of the other equipment seen in the book. I owe all of them a debt of thanks; as always, their work is of an unusually high standard of excellence.
Above all, my greatest gratitude is due to my wife Alison, who has contributed a great deal to the research contained in this book and has also shared the hardships of the many excursions around Europe necessary during the preparation of this and previous books. These often involved sleeping in the car or in freezing tents at Jena and Leipzig in October, not to mention Austerlitz in December!

AVAILABILITY OF PHOTOGRAPHS
From each of the photographs in this book a limited edition of only five 10in x 8in prints, plus one of each enlarged to 20in x 16in, are available for private purchase. Details from: Five Star Photography, 34 North Lodge Terrace, Darlington DL3 6LY, England.

CONTENTS

FOREWORD

BY DAVID G. CHANDLER,

HONORARY PRESIDENT, NAPOLEONIC ASSOCIATION

It may be an overused cliché to remark that every picture is worth a thousand words, but it is apt for *The Napoleonic Soldier* – Stephen Maughan's excellent photographs do indeed evoke a bygone age with great vividness, although his words, too, are evidence of many years of deep study of the primary sources.

The modern technique of photographic historical reconstruction is also in keeping with fine traditions from the past. The Napoleonic period, with its glorious uniforms and dramatic tableaux of dashing cavalry, stoic infantry and solid artillery, has always fascinated artists, from Jean-Louis Meissonier, Henri-Felix Philippoteaux and Jean-Baptist Detaille of the French school, to the Dighton brothers, Lady Butler, Ernest Croft and Richard Caton Woodville. Like them, Stephen Maughan is not so seduced by the colour and drama of his subject that he forgets the horrors of actual warfare – the dead and wounded have their place in these pages, too.

As a British military historian, having worked for over 33 years at the Royal Military Academy, Sandhurst, I have been deeply fascinated by our own "red coat" traditions of this period; but I soon decided to become a so-called French officer in our early Napoleonic Association, which has developed so interestingly over almost twenty years. I chose the French side of the hill for two reasons. First, it was a challenge to be a Frenchman at Sandhurst of all places; and above all, I feel that I owe something to Napoleon Bonaparte for my writing of *Campaigns of Napoleon* and other books on this period.

To end, let me quote Oliver Cromwell. For me Stephen Maughan might be called a "plain russet-coated captain, that knew what he fights for and loves what he knows". We are fortunate in having his strong abilities both as a fine photographer and also as a military historian. I commend to you his latest interesting volume.

ECHOES OF GLORY

Every French soldier carries in his cartouch box his baton of a Marshal of France; the only question is how to get it out.
(Elzéar Blaze)

Afterthe Napoleonic Wars had ended on the field of Waterloo, and the man whose name embodied this virtual world war of almost 20 years lay "chained to the rock of St.Helena", he described that final battle as "a concurrence of unexampled fatalities – a day not to be comprehended. Was there treason? Or was there only misfortune?"

Throughout the wars of Napoleon there had been plenty of both, along with glory, drama, and massive suffering, as the nations of Europe fought a titanic struggle to redress the balance capsized by the French Revolution, the torch of which Napoleon usurped and bent to his own will. During all of this the individuals who bore the brunt of national policies were, of course, the private soldiers, NCOs and regimental officers who had to carry out the designs of kings and ministers – often at the cost of their lives. It was they, along with the civilian populace in the theatres of war, who paid for all the glory with their pain and blood.

However, the most obvious trap awaiting any student of history is the thoughtless judgement of men and events against the conditions and values of our own time. This was a very different age, and the surviving writings of those who lived through it make it quite clear that they held different attitudes towards hardship and suffering, which were formed in the late 18th century. Death was a commonplace for all classes of civil society; infant mortality was shockingly high, life expectancy was low, and before the birth of modern medicine many diseases and serious injuries meant inevitable and sometimes agonising death. Particularly among the lower classes who provided the common soldiers everyday life was precarious enough, in those years before the link was established between clean public water supplies, efficient sanitation, and the avoidance of epidemic disease.

Two hundred years ago the modern Western emphasis on the overriding importance of the individual would have seemed puzzling. (This was not merely a matter of class indifference; before the Industrial Revolution and the later decline in religious belief the relationship between the classes was far from sentimental, but it was an essentially rural

Monument to the fallen French eagle at Waterloo, symbolising the end of Napoleon's reign as the terror of the monarchies of Europe. It was here on 18 June 1815 that the final curtain came down upon the Napoleonic Wars.

relationship informed by shared experience.) After Napoleonic battles the dying and the dead alike were routinely searched and robbed by the survivors, and not only by enemy survivors. The corpses of the common soldiers were stripped and slung into common gravepits; many of the fallen – as during the Russian campaign – were simply left lying where they fell for the carrion birds and beasts. Officers often fared no better, although they might at least warrant a memorial plaque in their local church. Even when individual officers could be distinguished among the cadavers they were often still buried in mass graves, such as the 15 officers and one warrant officer who lie in a Waterloo vault in Brussels City Cemetery.

The expectation that one would have to suffer serious pain at some point in ones life was commonplace in an age before mankind even dreamt of the almost universally available analgesics and anaesthetics of the 20th century. Stoic individuals left many remarkable contemporary accounts of amputations and the treatment of other severe wounds. George Napier felt that he had not borne the amputation of his arm as well as he ought to have done: "…for I made noise enough when the knife cut through my skin and flesh. It is no joke, I assure you, but still it was a shame to say a word, as it is of no use. Staff Sergeant Guthrie cut it off, however for want of light and from the number of amputations he had already performed, and their circumstances, his instruments were blunted, so it was a long time before the thing was finished, at least

(Above) The Lion Mound (Butte de Lion) seen from the road behind the Fallen Eagle, looking north and west from the French to the Allied lines. Built shortly after the battle to commemorate the position where the Prince of Orange was wounded during the fighting, its height of 125 feet was attained by excavating the slight ridge along which the centre of Wellington's army had been drawn up on 18 June. Unfortunately for later historians, the shifting of this vast amount of soil altered the topography; Wellington later remarked wryly that the building of the mound had "ruined my battlefield."

(Opposite top) Whenever possible Wellington's defensive dispositions always employed a reverse slope to protect his troops from the stronger French artillery. Here a small section of the reverse slope at Waterloo survives at the rear (north) of the chateau of Hougoumont. Most of the trees in the orchards and woods around Hougoumont have long gone, along with the ridge which Wellington's men defended.

twenty minutes, and the pain was great. I then thanked him for his kindness, having sworn at him like a trooper while he was at it, to his great amusement."

For officers and men alike such nightmare ordeals were faced without anaesthetic and in the most unsanitary conditions imaginable – with the writhing patient held down on a bloody table improvised from a door or a few planks, often in a reeking stable or a hastily cleared cottage, lit only by candle lanterns, and with a growing heap of amputated limbs piling up a few feet away. Again and again this scene was repeated after every one of hundreds of battles and skirmishes; medical knowledge was primitive, but doctors knew by empirical experience that only the bone saw offered a reasonable chance of recovery from major injury to a limb. That so many men did indeed recover from such wounds and their treatment argues a toughness of both body and mind which is normally found today only in the Third World.

★ ★ ★

Armies of hundreds of thousands of men marched on foot or rode on horseback and unsprung horse-drawn wagons for many hundreds of miles in successive campaigning seasons, back and forth across Europe. Metalled roads were few; in wet weather the passage of an army churned the mud into a morass deep enough to suck a man's shoes from his feet, and in summer the choking dust drew the moisture out of a man until he was a dried-up husk. On the retreat from

Moscow in 1812 the French froze to death along the same roads on which, a few months before, the summer sun had reduced them to drinking horses' urine from puddles in the baked ruts.

The logistics of Napoleonic armies were more or less unreliable, and even the most professional of them were often unable to get basic rations of bread and meat up to the men with any regularity; some – notably the French – were generally expected to fend for themselves when campaigning in enemy territory. Unless billeted in a town campaigning soldiers often slept on the ground under the open sky; apart from the obvious hardships of the weather, casual field sanitation must often have led men to drink bad water. Siege camps and other large, prolonged encampments in any one area were notoriously vulnerable to diseases like cholera, typhus and enteric fever; but daily deaths on the march from illness, heatstroke or simple exhaustion were also commonplace.

As a campaign progressed horses as well as men suffered increasingly. The British General Robert Ballard Long reported during the Peninsular War that "Since we left Albe de Tormes my brigade is minus 80 horses, and 5 or 6 is still the daily average loss. They have not had a pound of grain of any kind each per diem for the last 14 days, and with all this work and fatigue, have had only leaves, or a scanty bite of sour grass to support nature." In other armies, with less of a tradition of regular unsaddling and daily care of horses than the British, the mounts and teams died in their thousands from lack of proper forage and from general neglect under the harsh conditions of a prolonged campaign.

★ ★ ★

The tactics of the period, governed by the available weapons technology, seldom allowed fighting from concealment; so the concept of camouflage was almost entirely absent. The soldiers of Napoleonic armies were dressed in uniforms of as many brave distinguishing colours as could be devised and made permanent (or not) by the dyes of the period (many of the relatively few surviving uniforms have changed colour over the years). The appearance of a Napoleonic army was usually spectacular, at least at the beginning of a campaign when the regiments had recently been refitted. It did not take long for this impression to disintegrate, however; bad weather and the wear and tear of campaign life soon ruined any uniform exposed to them.

After Waterloo, with its knee-deep mud, Cavalié Mercer of the Royal Horse Artillery describes how "the Greys and Inniskillings were mere wrecks - the former, I think did not muster 200 men, and the latter, with no greater strength, presented a sad spectacle of disorganisation and bad discipline; they had lost more than half their appointments; some had helmets, some had none; many had the skull cap, but with the crest cut or broken off; some were on their own large horses, others on little ones they had picked up; belts there were on some; many were without, not only belts, but also canteens and haversacks."

Captain Elzéar Blaze of the Grand Army expressed the simple truth in relation to the French, but it applied equally to all other Napoleonic armies: "But the Emperor, who had us always sleeping in the open - how could he have expected to have a fine looking army with soldiers dressed as clowns?"

Some élite regiments took a pride in their appearance even on campaign, however; Blaze went on to mention that the Imperial Guard looked magnificent and rendered great services even if they were regarded with jealousy by the Line troops for their extra pay and many privileges. He cited an example of this attitude:

"We were on the march; a baggage wagon, drawn by four mules, attempted to cross our column. The soldiers, passing in succession before the noses of the poor beasts, took a malicious pleasure in blocking their progress because they belonged to the Imperial Guard. One soldier called out in a jeering way, 'Come on, soldiers of the Line, make way for the mules of the Guard!' 'Bah!', responded another, 'those are donkeys.' ...' Well, even if they are donkeys, what's the difference? Don't you know that the Guard's donkeys have the rank of mules?'"

Things were little different in the Russian army. General Kutuzov had occasion to chide a badly dressed horseman he encountered, with the words "What kind of scum are you?" The reply was "Captain of General Staff Brosin, quartermaster of the 1st Cavalry Corps."

Like those of the other major combatant nations, troops of the Russian Guards could put on a fine appearance when required. Both Prussian and Russian Guardsmen were in general taller than their French equivalents due to the far more stringent entrance qualifications demanded by the Emperor of the French for his Guard. Admission to the lat-

ter was restricted to men who had performed heroic individual actions or who had at least fought in several campaigns; most other nation's guardsmen were selected for imposing looks alone. Jean-Roch Coignet, then a private soldier in the Grenadiers à Pied de la Garde, recalled how guardsmen of the Russian and French armies met and mingled during the peace negotiations after Friedland:

"We marched out in corps to meet this fine guard, which was to arrive by company. We each offered an arm to one of the giants, and as there were more of us than of them, two of us offered [an arm to each of them]. They were so tall they might have used us as walking sticks. As for me, the smallest of all, I had one of them all to myself. I was obliged to look up to see his face. I looked like a little boy beside him."

★ ★ ★

At a distance of some 200 years we can look back upon the Napoleonic period with an interest and fascination based upon the many period memoirs and surviving items of uniform and equipment. Faced with the testimony of the men who fought in those wars, we cannot refuse to take at face value their perceptions – many did respond proudly to the martial splendour of those armies, and many did believe that the chance of military glory was worth the risk of death. Our own age has different values, and we cannot separate the heroic spectacle from what we know of the terror and horror of a Napoleonic battlefield.

The soldiers of those days stood facing one another at short range in large formed bodies of troops, and both dealt and received death and mutilating wounds in equal measure until the morale of one side broke and they drained away, "like rain through a grate." The ghastly carpet which this process left spread over the battlefields of Europe obviously cannot be reproduced in the photographs which illustrate this book; but it has been our intention to explore both sides of this particular coin, by the combination of photographic reconstruction and the words of those who were there.

(Right) Monument to the soldiers of France who died in the unsuccessful attacks on Hougoumont. Napoleon entrusted Honoré Comte Reille, commander of his II Corps, with the task of providing a diversionary attack against the Allied right flank at Hougoumont to draw troops away from Wellington's centre so that the decisive blow could be struck there by d'Erlon's I Corps. Although no specific orders had been given to take the chateau itself Napoleon's brother Jerome, in command of the 6th Infantry Division of II Corps, decided that it was the key to the right flank of Wellington's position. He repeatedly hurled his division – the 1st Light and 1st, 2nd and 3rd Line Infantry – against the loop-holed walls of the burning manorhouse, its outbuildings and yard; but the desperate defenders managed to hold out, in fighting which came to hand-to-hand when men of Bachelu's 5th Division broke into the farmyard. Even if these costly assaults had succeeded there were plentiful Allied infantry waiting in reserve beyond the ridge above Hougoumont. Eventually over 12,000 Frenchmen were committed against around 2,000 defenders; but the diversion failed, as Wellington refused to weaken his centre and was able to throw back d'Erlon's attack.

The modern main road south from Brussels crosses the Waterloo battle-field, and passes immediately beside the strong walled farm of La Haye Sainte. A plaque (inset) commemorates its capture by light infantry and sappers from Donzelot's 2nd Division of d'Erlon's I Corps. Standing reading it, only feet from the rush of heavy traffic, gives the visitor little hint of the desperate fighting for these buildings on 18 June 1815, when they formed an important bastion thrust forward from the centre of Wellington's main line.

La Haye Sainte was stoutly defended by veteran German troops: the green-jacketed riflemen of Major George Baring's 2nd Light Battalion of the King's German Legion, detached from Colonel Christian von Ompteda's 2nd KGL Brigade. Two companies of the 1st Light Bn KGL and the Light Company of the 5th Line Bn, led by Captain von Wurmb, also aided in the defence, along with 150 Nassau troops from General August von Kruse's brigade.

Private Frederick Lindau of the 2nd Light Bn was positioned guarding the small door of the barn and from

there covered the main entrance. Major Baring repeatedly ordered him to retire after he suffered two head wounds which bled profusely; Lindau replied that "he would be a scoundrel that deserted you, so long as his head is on his shoulders." He was later taken prisoner (and relieved of a large purse of gold which he had previously taken from a Frenchman).

Private Dahrendorf suffered three bayonet wounds, but was still among the first to assist in quenching the fire that broke out; he remained in the farm to the last, having his leg shattered by a case shot when the survivors finally retreated to the ridge. Private Lindhorst helped defend a breach which the French had made in the wall of the farmyard, and when the ammunition ran out he continued to hold his post, fighting at first with his sword-bayonet, then with a large stick, and at last with a brick which he had torn out of the wall.

Major Baring recalled: "Never had I felt myself so elevated - but never also placed in so painful a position, where honour contended with a feeling for the safety of my men, who had given me

such unbounded proof of their confidence." He goes on to praise the courage of the French attackers; despite the KGL's accurate fire, they could not "prevent them from throwing themselves against the walls, and endeavouring to wrest the weapons from the hands of my men through the loopholes."

It was not until after the defenders' ammunition was exhausted that the survivors attempted to retreat from the farmyard to the British-held ridge via the rear garden. In an attempt to cover this withdrawal the farmhouse was left occupied; but the passage to the interior of the house was very narrow, and while crowding in to make their escape many of the defenders were overtaken by the French attackers. Ensign Frank, who had already been wounded, was assailed here by two Frenchmen. He sabred one of them but his second attacker shot him, breaking his left arm. Frank sought safety in an inner room of the house, hiding behind a bed. Two of his comrades were also in the room, but when the French burst in they were both shot down. Frank remained hidden until the farmhouse was recaptured.

During the attempted break-out to the Allied line Captain Holtzermann and Lieutenant Tobin were captured. Major Hans von den Buesche (1st Light Bn) had his right arm shattered – it later had to be amputated – and Lieutenant Carey was wounded. Even after regaining the hollow road behind the farm and joining up with the 1st Light Bn the survivors continued to suffer casualties. Captain Henry von Marschalck was struck down, along with Lieutenant Albert; Captain von Gilsa was severely wounded in the right arm; and Lieutenants Wolrabe, Leonhardt, Behre, Miniussir, Koester, Gibson, Genzkow, Heise, Kessler, Luidam, Riefkugal, Timmann, Knop, Meyer and Captain Wynecken were all wounded, most of them severely. It has been said that of the 400-odd original defenders of La Haye Sainte only 42 reached the Allied line safely.

Major Baring himself had many narrow escapes; four musket balls entered the cloak which was strapped to the front of his saddle, another shot knocked his hat off, and when he dismounted to retrieve it another ball hit his saddle.

THE BACKBONE OF THE ARMY

After firing a volley as soon as the enemy were within shot, we pushed on with fixed bayonets and that hearty "Hurrah" peculiar to British soldiers. (Ensign Reece Howell Gronow)

Numerically and tactically, infantry were the backbone of a Napoleonic army. The spectacular cavalry were essential for screening, reconnaissance and raiding, and might turn the outcome of a battle by a heroic and brilliantly timed charge. The artillery was employed at this period with an increasing flexibility and sophistication which often overcame the limitations of its equipment; but although it could be lethal, it was essentially a preparatory arm, softening up the enemy before the attack. The Napoleonic general's base of fire was the solid mass of his infantry; and the battle was not won until the survivors of that infantry trudged forward, musket in hand, to take and occupy the ground.

Soldiers were drawn from many disparate areas of civilian life, but overwhelmingly from the rural peasantry. In the armies of mainland Europe the normal method of filling the ranks was a mixture of volunteer recruitment, the hiring of foreign mercenaries, and conscription – forced enlistment, usually by some ballot system under which a locality had to provide a certain number of fit men of a specified age group. In many armies draftees who had the means were allowed to buy their way out by paying a substitute to take their place.

The character of the infantry produced by conscription varied considerably. Prussia, for instance, with a small population, recognised the value of releasing men back into civilian life after a period of service, thus creating a trained reserve for mobilisation at need without stripping the national economy of valuable workers. Austria-Hungary ruled a large multinational empire across which terms of service varied widely; conscripts served alongside volunteers, and many mercenaries from other German-speaking states. Russia, vast and autocratic, simply took a certain number of illiterate serfs annually from each region, conscripting them for life.

The French soldier of the old regime had been a long-term volunteer professional. General conscription – the *levée en masse* – was introduced in a wave of patriotic fervour when the other powers moved to strangle the infant Revolution in the 1790s; but the armies which won Napoleon's early victories still had a good proportion of volunteers, formed around a backbone of old regulars. Under the Consulate some conscripts were released after ten years; but as time passed and losses mounted conscripts came to make up by far the greatest proportion of the French army, alongside soldiers from countries which the French had either occupied or forced into alliance. Basically any able-bodied, unmarried Frenchman who was not the sole support of elderly parents or orphaned brothers and sisters was liable for conscription in his twentieth year, for an unlimited period in wartime.

Unlike the Royal Navy – whose "press gangs" roamed the coastal regions to sweep up landsmen and merchant seamen alike – the regular regiments of the British army remained an all-volunteer force throughout the Napoleonic Wars. The part-time home defence Militia were raised by a compulsory ballot

A British redcoat as he would have appeared in the Peninsular War – the campaigns in Portugal and Spain between 1808 and 1814, which made Wellington's name as a general, and restored the British army's reputation as a highly professional battle-winning force after two generations of decline.

His headgear is the "stovepipe" shako of black felt which replaced an earlier leather type from 1806; most Line regiments wore this universal pattern of brass plate. The black cockade is pinned in place by a regimental button, the IX identifying the 9th or Norfolk Regiment of Foot; it is surmounted by the white-over-red worsted plume worn by the eight centre or "Battalion" companies of each battalion (the other two "flank" companies of picked men being the Light and Grenadier companies, which wore green and white plumes respectively).

Each regiment had two or more battalions, the 1st Bn available for service abroad and the 2nd theoretically remaining at the home depot, recruiting and training replacements for the 1st. (During the Napoleonic Wars a number of 2nd Bns. were also sent overseas, and some regiments raised 3rd Battalions.) The entire regiment was distinguished by facing colours worn on the collar, shoulder straps and cuffs of the red jacket or coatee – see the Appendix for a list of these; and by the shape, spacing, and patterns of coloured lines in the loops of white tape applied to the buttonholes. A black stock – officially of leather, to keep the chin up – was worn at the throat.

(*Left*) *British redcoats stand guard outside the period gaol at the reconstructed Napoleonic dockyard at Hartlepool, built to house the restored frigate HMS* Trincomalee. *These are men of the 68th (Durham) Light Infantry; the Light regiments were distinguished by green shako plumes, tufted cloth "wings" sewn to the shoulders, and a buglehorn shako badge (the flank companies of Line battalions also wore the wings). The 68th had deep green facings, and square-ended loops set in pairs. For active service the infantrymen wore hard-wearing grey trousers over – or instead of – their regulation white breeches, and short grey or black spat-type gaiters over their laced shoes. For this sentry duty they wear their basic accoutrements: a pair of broad whitened leather crossbelts supporting a cartridge pouch and a bayonet scabbard behind the right and left hips respectively.*

system, but except at times of great national emergency militia-men could not be drafted into Line regiments against their will. Those who could be tempted to exchange into the Line were prized recruits, since they were already at least partly trained, and volunteers were offered bounties of up to 12 guineas – more than eight months' pay.

Regiments were allotted recruiting areas, and from time to time they would send out recruiting parties to "beat up" for volunteers – the phrase referred to the merry drumming which always heralded their approach to a market place or country fair. The party comprised an officer, two sergeants, a drummer and a few soldiers, all turned out in their best military finery and eager to attest to the benefits and adventures to be enjoyed by those likely lads who had the spirit to take the King's red coat.

The lure of a cash bounty of about £2.12s., along with generous quantities of free ale, ensured that they seldom returned to their battalions without a number of recruits who had been induced to accept the King's Shilling. Upon being

pronounced fit after a cursory examination by a district sur-geon, and having signed the Articles of War, the recruit was now marched off to his regimental depot, and his military career could commence. As for the promised bounty, that mostly disappeared to pay for his "necessaries"; since these included two guineas deducted for his knapsack, the recruit often began his confusing new life with only a hangover to remember his enlistment by.

The surviving records of a few British infantry companies and recruiting parties allow us a glimpse of the typical redcoat of the Napoleonic Wars, though they obviously do not provide a statistically reliable sample. The majority of recruits were of English birth, but there were many Irishmen and Scotsmen serving in nominally English regiments. Most recruits were listed as labourers – which at that date meant farmworkers – with a noticeable minority of skilled workmen such as weavers and frame-knitters, and a scattering of other trades such as tai-lors, shoemakers and metal workers. Of 100 men recruited for the 98th Foot in 1793 we find that 66 were between 5ft 4ins

(Above) The 68th Durhams in action. Although light infantry were often employed in the main battle line, fighting in solid formation like the rest of the Foot, they were also trained to skirmish ahead of the main line in open order. On these occasions they operated much like Riflemen (see page 33 et seq), making use of cover and firing by turns, to harass and disorganise the advancing enemy.

(Right) When the 71st (Glasgow Highland) Light Infantry were selected to convert to that role the kilt was – inexplicably – considered unsuitable for skirmishers, and the 71st were ordered to retain only "such portions of the Highland dress as would not interfere with light infantry duties." In keeping with their origins the rankers wore a dark blue shako with a band of Highland dicing around the base and, in some sources, a tuft or toorie on the top, made by stiffening a Highland bonnet. Note that the 71st were one of the buff-faced regiments which traditionally wore buff rather than whitened crossbelts. Another Highland distinction was their use of bagpipers.

During the advance on the evening of Waterloo Lieutenant William Torriano led some of the 71st in capturing a French cannon and turned it upon its French owners. A soldier of the 71st (possibly Thomas Howell) gives us a graphic account of what it was like to face a French attack column:

"We marched out two miles to meet the enemy, formed line and lay under cover of a hill for about an hour, until they came to us. We gave them one volley and three cheers – three distinct cheers. Then all was as still as death. They came upon us crying and shouting to the very points of our bayonets. Our awful silence and determined advance they could not stand. They put about and fled without much resistance. At this charge we took thirteen guns and one general. We advanced into a hollow and formed again ... The French came down upon us again. We gave them another specimen of a charge as effectual as our first and pursued them three miles.

"In our first charge I felt my mind waver. A breathless sensation came over me. The silence was appalling. I looked alongst the line. It was enough to assure me. The steady, determined scowl of my companions assured my heart and gave me determination."

and 5ft 9ins tall; 21 were less than 5ft 4ins, and only three were 5ft 10ins or taller. Of these same 100 recruits 33 were aged between 30 and 35, 31 were between 18 and 24, 19 were between 25 and 29, and 17 were between 15 and 17 years of age. The average may have got younger as the wars progressed; the roll of a company at Waterloo in 1815 shows that less than ten per cent had more than four years' regular service at that date – though 55 per cent of that particular company had volunteered from the Militia.

Daily pay in the foot regiments of the Line amounted to: private, 1 shilling; drummer, 1s.1¾d.; corporal, 1s.2¼d.; sergeant, 1s.6¾d.; quartermaster sergeant & sergeant major, 2s.0¾d. But out of his weekly pay of 7s. the soldier had stoppages deducted of 4s. for his mess arrangements; and 1s.6d. for other necessaries provided at his own expense, for instance black cloth gaiters, 4s.; breeches, 6s.6d.; worm turnscrew, picker and brush for cleaning musket (per five years), 1s.3d.; emery, brick dust and oil for cleaning metal equipment, 2s.6d. per annum. Any lost equipment also had to be paid for. It is not difficult to understand why soldiers routinely searched the pockets of battlefield corpses. But equally, in an age when an unemployed man might literally starve in a ditch, it is easy to see the appeal of any wage at all as long as it came with two square meals a day, clothing, and a roof.

To supplement the willing volunteers recruiting officers were happy to enlist petty criminals of all kinds straight from the dock of a magistrate's court; the alternatives presented to such men encouraged the rapid choice of service in His Majesty's forces. Indeed, in the minds of most of the populace, a soldier was regarded as little better than a criminal – and it must be admitted that they often earned this reputation by their drunken and violent behaviour. It must be remembered, however, that this was still a brutal age, when anyone over the age of seven years could be hung for a theft of five shillings; so not all criminals enlisted into the army were as bad as might be imagined, some being guilty of little more than petty theft in order to eat. Others, inevitably, were truly of the kind of whom Wellington said that "gin was the spirit of their patriotism."

Discipline under the conditions of the day was hard to enforce; and given the public's suspicion and hostility towards soldiers, it was necessary even on home service to set an occasional example of the fate which could befall malefactors. One member of a firing squad recalled a military execution organised on such a grand scale that one wonders if it were not a relatively rare event:

"As the execution would be a good hint to us young 'uns, there were four lads picked out of our corps to assist in this piece of duty, myself being one of the number chosen. Besides

The 42nd (Royal Highland) Regiment of Foot – traditionally known as the Black Watch, from its dark tartan plaid and its mid-18th century origins in the government-paid independent companies which policed the Scottish Highlands. Wellington's Highland regiments were renowned for their fighting prowess; and their men were generally more sober, more devout, and better behaved than the English and Irish regiments. Their uniforms comprised the red jacket with the kilt in regimental pattern tartan; cut from a single length of material with a central pleated section, it could be tailored by varying the number of pleats. (Three and a half yards of cloth were allowed for a soldier's kilt and four yards for a sergeant's – modern kilts need seven or eight yards for their deep folds of knife pleating.) The headdress was the blue Kilmarnock bonnet with a diced band, dressed with black ostrich feathers and sometimes with a laced-on peak. These soldiers of the grenadier company have shoulder wings, and a red cap cockade with grenade and sphinx badges, the latter awarded to mark distinguished service in Egypt in 1801.

The 42nd served in the Peninsula in 1808-09, then in the Walcheren expedition in Holland (where many soldiers perished of fever), returning to the Peninsula for the 1812-14 campaigns. During the 1815 Hundred Days campaign in Belgium they fought with great distinction at Quatre-Bras and Waterloo. After Waterloo their exotic costume made them popular with ladies and artists alike on the streets of Paris, though many illustrations dating from this period are fanciful in the extreme.

One corporal of the 42nd (in The personal narrative of a private soldier in the 42nd Highlanders) recommended the ideal method of remaining awake on outpost or piquet duty: "After much fatigue of marching for a day and a night, with hardly any sleep, always keep moving about, and never sit down at night, or rest against any thing; but prick themselves with pins, as I have done often, and wash their eyes with their own water. There is nothing either disgusting or unpleasant in this: I have done it often, and found it the best antidote against drowsiness."

these men, four soldiers from three other regiments were ordered on the firing party, making sixteen in all. The place of execution was Portsdown Hill, near Hilsea Barracks, and the different regiments assembled must have composed a force of about fifteen thousand men, having been assembled from the Isle of Wight, from Chichester, Gosport and other places. The sight was very imposing and appeared to make a deep impression on all there. As for myself ... I would have given a good round sum ... to have been in any situation rather than the one in which I now found myself ....

"When all was ready, we were moved to the front, and the culprit was brought out. He made a short speech to the parade, acknowledging the justice of his sentence, and that drinking and evil company had brought the punishment upon him. He behaved himself firmly and well, and did not seem at all to flinch. After being blindfolded, he was desired to kneel down behind a coffin, which was placed on the ground, and the drum major of the Hilsea depot giving us an expressive glance, we immediately commenced loading. This was done in the deepest silence, and the next moment we were primed and ready. There was then a dreadful pause for a few moments, and the drum major, again looking towards us, gave the signal before agreed upon (a flourish of his cane), and we levelled and fired.

"We had been previously enjoined to be steady, and take

good aim, and the poor fellow, pierced by several balls, fell heavily upon his back; and as he lay, with his arms pinioned to his sides, I observed that his hands wavered for a few moments, like the fins of a fish when in the agonies of death. The drum major also observed the movement, and making another signal, four of our party immediately stepped up to the prostrate body, and placing the muzzles of their pieces to his head, fired and put him out of his misery.

"The different regiments then fell back by companies, and the word being given to march past in slow time, when each company came in line with the body the word was given to mark time and then eyes left, in order that we might all observe the terrible example."

This passage comes from the *Recollections of Rifleman Harris*, who served in the British 95th Rifles; but there are many other references from all the other armies of the period to the use of capital and corporal punishment, and a remarkably similar execution in the French army is described by Elzéar Blaze.

When time permitted, the punishments inflicted in some European armies could reach a certain refinement of sadism. In the American army which fought against the British in the War of 1812 minor offences could be punished by a spell astride the wooden horse – a traditional German punishment, which presumably found its way to America with the German

HIGHLANDERS IN BATTLE

(Right & opposite) Sergeants of the 42nd Highlanders; like their officers, Highland sergeants wore their sash over the shoulder rather than around the waist in English style. The polearm carried by battalion and grenadier company sergeants – variously called a halberd or half-pike – was a survival from earlier centuries, and by this period was used more often for aligning the ranks than as a weapon.

At Quatre-Bras on 16 June 1815 the 42nd were approached by lancers whom Sergeant Alexander McEween's officer took for Allied troops. McEween said he was sure they were French lancers, whom he had previously seen when a prisoner of war. He proposed to fire at them to see how they reacted; when he did so they immediately advanced on the 42nd. Sergeant Anton takes up the story:

"We instantly formed a rallying square [i.e. a solid square, back to back]; no time for particularity; every man's piece was loaded, and our enemies approached at full charge; the feet of their horses seemed to tear up the ground. Our skirmishers having been impressed with the same opinion that these were Brunswick cavalry, fell beneath their lances and few escaped death or wounds; our brave Colonel fell at this time, pierced through the chin until the point of the lance reached the brain. Captain (now Major) Menzies fell, covered with wounds, and a momentary conflict took place over him; he was a powerful man and hand to hand more than a match for six ordinary men. The Grenadiers, whom he commanded, pressed round to save or avenge him, but fell beneath the enemies' lances. Of all descriptions of cavalry, certainly the lancers seem the most formidable to infantry, as the lance can be projected with considerable precision, and with deadly effect, without bringing the horse to the point of the bayonet; and it was only by the rapid and well directed fire of musketry that these formidable assailants were repulsed.

"… The lancers overtook two companies in the act of completing the square. Several of the 42nd were cut off, but a portion of the lancers became hemmed inside the square by the remainder of those two companies, and were instantly bayoneted."

Highland regiments had already won a great reputation in the Peninsula, in actions such as that at Toulouse the previous year, also recounted by Sergeant Anton:

"The light companies of the division advanced beyond the road, and maintained a very unequal skirmish with the enemy, who lay securely posted behind their breastworks and batteries, and in their redoubts, from all of which they took the most deadly aim. The 61st Regiment was ordered forward to support the skirmishers, and became the marked object of the enemies' batteries, from which incessant showers of grape cut down that corps by sections, whilst Soult was perhaps not losing a man, being so safely sheltered from our musketry."

The mauled 61st were withdrawn and, emboldened, the French advanced in great strength. The 42nd were now ordered to take one of the enemys redoubts: "Our Colonel was a brave man, but there are moments when a well timed manoeuvre is of more advantage than courage. The regiment stood on the road with its front exactly to the enemy, and if the left wing had been ordered forward, it could have sprung up the bank in line and dashed forward on the enemy at once. Instead of this, the Colonel faced the right wing to its right, countermanded in rear of the left, and when the leading rank cleared the left flank it was made to file up the bank, and as soon as it made its appearance the shot, shell and musketry poured in with deadly destruction; and in this exposed position we had to make a second countermarch, on purpose to bring our front to the enemy.

"These movements consumed much time, and by this unnecessary exposure exasperated the men to madness. The words Forward – double quick! dispelled the gloom, and forward we drove, in the face of apparent destruction. The field had been lately rough ploughed or under fallow, and when a man fell he tripped the one behind, thus the ranks were opening as we approached the point whence all this hostile vengeance proceeded; but the rush forward had received an impulse from desperation; the spring of the men's patience had been strained until ready to snap … In a minute every obstacle was surmounted; the enemy fled as we leaped over the trenches and mounds like a pack of noisy hounds in pursuit, frightening more by our wild hurrahs than actually hurting them by ball or bayonet."

The French advance continued, and Sergeant Anton's unit would soon be forced to retire. "Time would not permit of particularity, and a brisk independent fire was kept up with more noise than good effect by our small groups … Our muskets were getting useless by the frequent discharges and several of the men were having recourse to the French pieces that lay scattered about, and were equally unserviceable. Our number of effective hands was also decreasing and that of the approaching foe seemed irresistible.

"Two officers (Captain Campbell and Lieutenant Young) and about sixty of inferior rank were all that now remained without a wound of the right wing of the regiment … The flag was hanging in tatters, and stained with the blood of those who had fallen over it. The standard, cut in two, had been successively placed in the hands of three officers, who fell as we advanced; it was now borne by a sergeant, while the few remaining soldiers who rallied around it, defiled with mire, sweat, smoke and blood, stood ready to oppose with the bayonet the advancing column, the front files of which were pouring in destructive showers of musketry among our confused ranks.

"… The right wing of the regiment thus broken down and in disorder, was rallied by Captain Campbell (afterwards brevet Lieutenant-Colonel) and the adjutant (Lieutenant Young) on a narrow road, the steep banks of which served as a cover from the showers of grape that swept over our heads. In this contest, besides our Colonel, who was wounded as he gave the word of command Forward, the regiment lost, in killed and wounded, twenty officers, one sergeant-major and four hundred and thirty six of inferior rank."

Anton himself had had several close escapes: "a musket ball struck my halberd in line with my cheek, another passed between my arm and my side and lodged in my knapsack, another struck the handle of my sword, and a fourth passed through my bonnet and knocked it off my head. The company in which I was doing duty lost four officers, three sergeants and forty seven rank and file in killed and wounded." Anton mentions his sergeant-major, "as brave a man as ever entered a field. Sent to carry an order to the left hand company, and cautioned to stoop as he preceded, he considered this unmanly and never did he walk with a more upright, dauntless carriage of the body or a firmer step: it was his last march; a bullet pierced his brain and stretched him lifeless, without a sigh."

drillmasters employed by the Continental Congress. This comprised a narrow beam or plank set edgeways across trestles, astride which the victim was sat with his tied legs dangling beneath. A number of muskets were now strapped to his feet, both to keep him in position and to increase the weight pressing his groin down on his narrow perch.

Another widely used method was the picket, whereby the soldier was triced up by one hand to the top of a long, sturdy post driven into the ground. A small peg was hammered into the ground at the base of the post so that one of the man's bare heels could just reach it to help support his weight – but only at the cost of increasing agony to the heel. The *gantelope* or gauntlet was used all over Europe to punish such crimes as theft from comrades. The men formed up in two lines facing inwards and holding sticks; the offender, naked to the waist, was marched down this lane – with a sergeant's pike at his chest to prevent him moving too quickly – while each man in the lines was allowed (in theory) one blow.

Such imaginative foreign cruelties were not permitted in the British army. Yet while regarding picketing as an unacceptable torture such as Spaniards might inflict on their slaves, the British soldier was still able to regard ferocious floggings with a cat-o'-nine-tails, sometimes of hundreds of lashes, as a frightening but reasonable means of enforcing discipline.

When the discipline of an army in the field broke down into looting and disregard for authority, its effectiveness as a fighting force, and thus its very survival, was in peril. By the standards of the day Wellington was a reasonable and humane commander, always conscious of what he could realistically demand from his soldiers; but he was renowned for the strictness of the discipline he enforced. Elzéar Blaze recalled the unevenness of French discipline while on campaign: "But what I have ever disapproved, what was always a great affliction to me, was the severity with which pillage was punished one day, after it had been tacitly authorised for a month. From the moment the order was issued, woe betide him who disobeyed it! Next day he was no more." By contrast, Wellington's officers and men knew exactly where they stood, and many of their memoirs mention the punishments inflicted upon soldiers for murder, rape and theft. In the Peninsula it was especially important that Spanish co-operation was maintained, and the British army enforced a policy of paying for its supplies rather than appropriating them at bayonet-point in the manner of their French opponents.

The normal sanction in the British army was flogging, and when this was awarded in barracks or billets the offender was strapped to a tripod of sergeants' pikes and the battalion was paraded to witness punishment. One example of a flogging while on the march was recorded during the dreadful winter retreat to Corunna, when General Craufurd ordered one soldier 300 lashes for insubordination. The only difficulty was the lack of a tripod, since NCOs of the Rifles and Light Infantry did not carry pikes. They led the culprit to a slender ash tree, but he told them: "Don't trouble yourselves about tying me up, I'll take my punishment like a man". With that he folded his arms and braced himself, and received the whole 300 lashes without a murmur. When the flogging was over his wife covered him with his grey greatcoat, and as the retreat continued she carried the jacket, knapsack and pouch which his lacerated back could not support.

An hour later Craufurd again halted his men and intended to flog two more men who had been found guilty of leaving the column. Upon an intercession by their lieutenant-colonel Craufurd partially relented: "I will allow you this much: you shall draw lots, and the winner shall escape; but one of the two I am determined to make an example of." The two men then drew straws, the loser being tied to a tree and receiving 75 of his allotted 100 lashes before the general again relented and sent him back to his company.

Given the circumstances, the general was only doing what was necessary to prevent his rearguard from disintegrating; and "Black Bob" Craufurd was a popular commander. Rifleman Harris, who was present, agreed: "I who was there, and was besides a common soldier of the very regiment to which these men belonged, say it was quite necessary. No man but one formed of stuff like General Craufurd could have saved the brigade from perishing altogether; and if he flogged two he saved hundreds from death by his management."

On a rather lighter note, an interesting disciplinary item may be found in the Standing Orders for the Third West York Militia for 1809 – an order that after Divine Services "The men are to quit the church without noise, and are not to make water against the church nor in the churchyard, to the annoyance of any."

(Below) Early French Revolutionary infantry were hampered by a lack of training; a mass of keen but unschooled volunteers could charge, but could not carry out complex manoeuvres on the battlefield. To harness their enthusiasm they were originally organised in mixed regiments with two volunteer battalions flanking one battalion of pre-Revolutionary regular soldiers who provided a base of fire and manoeuvre. French armies also advanced in much more open order than their conventionally trained enemies, thus avoiding some of the effect of enemy volleys and cannon fire. They sent out large numbers of tirailleurs - skirmishers - to harass the enemy from close range until the bulk of infantry could be brought up close enough to mount one of their great attacks by massed assault columns. By the mid-1790s as many as one man in five were commonly used as skirmishers ahead of the main line. From 1804 skirmishers formed a permanent voltigeur company within each battalion, distinguished - as here - by yellow or buff collars and fringed green and yellow epaulettes. The fusilier or centre companies (four, from at least 1808) wore blue shoulder straps, and the grenadier company red epaulettes. From at least 1808 a regiment normally had four battle battalions, serving together, and one depot battalion.

(Above) The great victories of Napoleon's early career, including Austerlitz in 1805, were won by soldiers uniformed like this. The bicorn or tricorn hat or "felt" - originally simply a broad-brimmed slouch hat, with the brim fixed up in various ways to give a smarter appearance - had been the most widely worn military headgear of the 18th century. In Revolutionary France it was decorated with a cockade in the red, white and blue of the new Republic and with various plumes or tufts. The first Revolutionary armies wore a ragbag of different clothing, and many old white uniforms of the ancien régime survived for years; but gradually a new Republican uniform based on that of the Paris National Guard became generally available, in the new national colours of blue faced and piped with white and red. In the early years men and units had to shift for themselves as regards waistcoats, trousers and shoes; but in time white "smallclothes" and black gaiters became general issue. In an age before true mass production, with uniforms ordered by individual units from many dispersed suppliers, there were often small differences between regiments; but officially all French Line regiments wore the same uniform, undifferentiated by facing colours.

(Below) *Infantrymen of the later Napoleonic campaigns: a sergeant and a quartermaster-corporal of the 2nd fusilier company of a battalion of the 127eme de ligne, uniformed in accordance with the 1812 Bardin regulations. Since 1810 the brass shako plate had been simplified to this lozenge bearing the regimental number; coloured pompons identified the 1st to 4th fusilier companies of all battalions – dark green, sky blue, orange-pink and violet respectively. The Bardin reforms of 1812 shortened the coat to this closed* habit-veste, *and shortened the gaiters to below the knee. Non-commissioned rank was still identified by diagonal stripes on the forearms in yellow and gold.*

The 127th were formed in Hamburg in March 1811 from the Hamburg and Lübeck Civil Guards and the Hanoverian Legion along with conscripts and volunteers. This was one of a number of foreign regiments taken into the numbered French Line as Napoleon built up his Grande Armée for his planned invasion of Russia; officers were mainly French with a few bilingual Germans, and orders were to be given in French. Had he succeeded in Russia, one wonders how soon the identities of all other beaten or cowed Continental states would have been blurred into one huge, nominally French army for Napoleon's European superstate?

(Above) *The shako began to replace the bicorn from 1806; it was smarter and made the soldier look taller, and with its leather top, peak and side-bands and brass chinscales it gave some small protection against blows and cuts. It also lent itself to dressing with plates, plumes and festoons of plaited cords for an impressive appearance on parade. The 21st of the Line was one of many regiments to adopt this non-regulation but handsome plate with the Imperial eagle surmounting an Amazon shield; others had their own distinct patterns, like that of the 54th bearing an embossed profile bust of the Emperor. Fusiliers wore white cords; these hang to the right for a reason, and the jaunty angle of this shako worn by a 1st Company soldier is not an affectation. Both are to prevent cords and shako from interfering with the musket during drill sessions - it was carried on the left shoulder. The 21st was a veteran regiment which fought at Austerlitz, Jena, Eylau, Eckmühl, Wagram, Saragossa in Spain, Smolensk and Borodino in Russia, Dresden, and finally at Waterloo.*

(Left) *Voltigeur sergeant (note the yellow collar facing) of the 5th Italian Line in French service, c.1809 — one of seven Italian regiments which Napoleon sent to fight in Spain in 1808-13. In 1806-07 French infantry were ordered into white uniforms (on grounds of economy); obviously impractical, this only lasted for a year, but in the meantime the Italian regiments also received a version of it.*

(Below left & right) *When off duty both officers and men wore the comfortable and practical* bonnet de police, *apparently so called because it was originally worn when under military arrest or confinement to quarters. Later it became an offence to be in camp with the head uncovered, and the bonnet — in appropriate colours, and smartened up with lace, piping, tassels and badges — became the regulation forage cap for all classes of troops.*

(Opposite) *Enemy's eye view of a grim old "Grumbler" of Napoleon's élite regiment — a sergeant of the* Grenadiers à pied de la Garde Impériale *demonstrating bayonet drill. The tall black bearskin* (bonnet à poil) *was the traditional distinction of grenadier companies in many national armies. Those worn by the complete regiments of Grenadiers and Chasseurs which Napoleon formed for his Guard were particularly imposing; the mixed gold and red cords and epaulettes, like the gold lace stripes on his sleeve, identify this veteran's rank.*

Jean-Baptiste Barrès gives us the entry qualification for the Vélites or volunteer officer candidates of the Consular Guard: "To be possessed of some education, to belong to a respectable family, to be at least 5ft 2ins in height, at least twenty years of age, and to pay 200 francs mess money ... Our pay was 23 sous 1 centime per diem. Nine sous we gave to the mess, 4 went to the fund to provide underclothing and shoes, and the other 10 were given to us every ten days as pocket money. The fare was good and the pay enough to provide all absolute necessaries, but deductions were often made which were not always very scrupulously accounted for, and of which we dared not complain.

(Left) Older veterans who were still capable of light duties in static garrisons were often transferred from bataillons de bataille to so-called Invalid Battalions; or – like this avuncular figure – to the Gendarmerie. The gendarmes fulfilled police functions, providing route security and rounding up stragglers and deserters, and were sometimes deployed in strength to insecure areas as anti-partisan troops. In Spain the large numbers of fearless guerrilleros tied down several thousand gendarmes in foot and mounted units. The rear areas of an army were often full of lost or unauthorised personnel, some attempting to find and rejoin their units, others trying to leave the army altogether; and large numbers of camp-followers of every kind choked the roads and disrupted the passage of troops and supplies. The gendarmes acted as a kind of rudimentary traffic police, attempting to impose order on the chaos.

(Below) A pioneer (sapeur) of the 18eme de ligne, wearing the bearskin which also distinguished members of the battalion pioneer section, who were drawn from among the strongest members of the grenadier company. Other traditional distinctions include the full beard; the leather apron to protect the uniform; and the axe used for felling trees to clear the route of march, for building fortifications, or for general field engineering tasks. They carried special rooster-headed, saw-backed sabres, and other tools as required. With their impressive accoutrements and decorations the pioneers were also called upon to provide headquarters guards; and on the march they formed the head of the column along with the band and the Eagle standard and its guard. The decorations on the crossbelts were often supplemented with crossed axe sleeve badges.

(Right) Austrian Grenadiers of a German regiment during arms inspection. Unlike most other armies Austria-Hungary did not possess any Guard regiments for field deployment. The grenadier companies incorporated the best men in each infantry regiment (as in other armies); but the Austrians routinely grouped grenadier companies from several units to form separate grenadier battalions for tactical use.

The Hapsburg dynasty's widespread possessions filled the ranks of the army with Germans, Hungarians, Czechs, Croats, Slovaks, Poles, Ukrainians, Russians, Romanians, Italians and Belgians. Most infantry regiments were classed as either "German" (including Bohemian, Moravian, and Tyrolean) or "Hungarian" (including Croatian and Transylvanian troops); there were also Italian, Walloon, and Grenzer

(Balkan border) regiments. German regiments had two field battalions; each had six fusilier companies, plus a detachment of gunners to operate three 6pdr. guns. Hungarian regiments had three field battalions with assigned Line artillery. Both types of regiment had an additional grenadier division of two companies.

(Below) Fusiliers of a German regiment on the march; the NCO's shako in the foreground shows rank lace, and also the national field sign – an oak-leaf sprig. Each man carried an 18.3mm calibre musket with cartridge box (60 rounds) and bayonet, a sabre, a haversack, and one water bottle for every two men. A tent and a copper cooking kettle were provided for every five men, and an additional 36 rounds of ammunition per man were also transported by each battalion's 30 packhorses.

(Left) Most period armies considered that each infantryman should go into battle with 60 rounds of ammunition in his cartridge box; a trade-off had to be made between the weight of ammunition carried (about 10lbs or 4.5kg for 60 rounds) and the amount needed. It was said of the supremely practical Duke of Wellington. "Provided we brought our men into the field well appointed with sixty rounds of good ammunition each, he never looked to see whether their trousers were black, blue or grey."

(Above) The cartridge was a paper tube formed by rolling around a wooden rod; the round lead ball and a pre-measured charge of black powder were dropped into the tube, and the end twisted shut. These were vulnerable to damp and to being shaken around in the pouch; some form of rigid container, either of wood or tin, was normally provided, and the leather pouch was waterproofed.

(Above & left) Unlike the waxed cartridge boxes of the Line, those of the French Imperial Guard were lacquered, and the outer flaps furnished with brass eagle and grenade emblems; note also the inner flap, and the superior stitched edges of the crossbelts. The box accomodated an oil bottle, and the outer pocket spare flints and a stripping tool. Other regiments grumbled that Napoleon's "Immortals" were so often held back from battle in reserve that they hardly needed ammunition – hence the nickname. While the battle of Jena was being fought on 14 October 1806 the Grenadiers à Cheval were 36 hours march away and the Guard infantry were kept in reserve, causing the comment, "Look - his Horse Guard escorts the wagon train and his Foot Guard rounds up the pillagers, while the Line licks the Prussians!"

(Right) French dragoons carried an infantry musket during the Consulate period; when supplies were available under the Empire they gradually received Year IX or XI Dragoon pattern weapons like this example, which was 70mm shorter for ease of handling when on horseback. True cavalry carbines were usually carried with the muzzle downwards in a leather boot, but the dragoons carried their muskets with the butt in a boot and the muzzle up. In the field they could carry them slung over the rider's back, but this is possible for only short periods of time, when in the face of the enemy; with the constant motion of riding the long weapon soon chafed the soldier's skin raw.

This picture shows good detail of a classic flintlock action: the flint wrapped in lead foil or a leather patch for a good grip in the screw jaws of the cock; the priming pan covered by the spring-loaded frizzen, against whose surface the flint struck sparks into the pan as it knocked it forward; and the weapon carried at half cock for safety.

There was little difference between the flintlocks (or "firelocks", in the old-fashioned term) which were made by the combatant powers, although the Prussians introduced a sensible weather- and flash-shield around the priming pan, and a double-ended ramrod. Most Napoleonic muskets were around 4ft 8ins to 5ft long, with barrels around 40ins long and a bore of approximately .75in; they took powder charges of anything from 100 grains (about a quarter-ounce or 7g) upwards, and fired lead balls of about 1½oz (42g) weight.

(Below) All black powder weapons quickly foul up with black, sludgy residue after a few shots, clogging the touch hole by which the spark passes from the priming pan to the main charge in the barrel, and making it progressively harder to ram a ball down the bore. Misfires were frequent, and all soldiers had to carry a wire pricker to pick out the touch hole. A small wire brush was also often carried, to scour the burnt residue out of the pan, and was hung with the pricker from a coat button. Another cause of misfiring was a chipped or broken flint, and even the best flints needed replacing after about 30 shots.

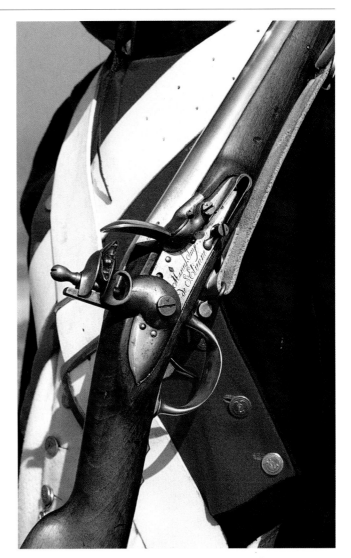

Loading a period musket was a similar procedure in all armies; the French drill manual identified 12 distinct steps. The paper cartridge was taken from the pouch, the end bitten off, and a little powder poured into the priming pan, which was then covered by snapping the frizzen back. The rest of the powder, the ball and the paper were then put into the muzzle and tamped home with the ramrod, and the ramrod returned to its place under the barrel. The cock was pulled back against its internal spring to full cock; and the musket was ready to fire.

(Left & below) *The corporal's musket drill is being supervised by a sergeant instructor; when he is deemed proficient he will, in turn, train a squad of conscripts. After the loss of hundreds of thousands of men in Russia, an army of 20-year-old conscripts were sent to the front for the 1813-14 campaigns in Saxony and France; the older soldiers called them "Marie-Louises", after the Emperor's*

young second wife, whose counter-signature appeared on the conscription decree. Due to the acute shortage of experienced NCOs caused by the terrible drain of casualties their training was often sadly overlooked. A conscript was seen in one action not even firing his musket, and upon being asked why he explained that no one had shown him how … .

(Right) Taking individual aim was usual for skirmishers or dismounted cavalry; but although the smoothbore musket threw its ball some hundreds of yards it was only accurate out to 50 yards. At 100 yards any soldier hit by an enemy who was actually aiming at him was considered "damned unlucky" - modern trials have shown that at that range it is hard to achieve

a ten-round group less than about 2ft 6ins across. The elevation of the musket was crucial, and many rounds sailed over the heads of their intended victims as the barrels were thrown up upon discharge. Tests in 1830 recorded a mean aim deviation at 100 yards range of no less than 5ft horizontally and 6ft vertically.

(Below) These KGL light infantrymen are firing Baker rifles, but the effect of the detonation of the priming is identical with any flintlock weapon. It is impossible for even an experienced man not to flinch and blink when the powder flares in front of his face; and the brief "hangfire" before the main charge goes off is long enough for this to upset the aim. Note the sparks flying in all directions.

(Right) Due to the short accurate range of the flintlock smoothbore the only way to inflict enough casualties on an opponent was to fire en masse, producing a shotgun effect against a formed body of the enemy. Analysis of late 18th and early 19th century battles suggests that opposing ranks exchanged volleys at an average of just over 60 yards range, closing to 30 yards during an attack. To deliver effective fire battalions had to be drawn up shoulder to shoulder; the allotted width per man was 22ins in the British army, 26ins in the French and 27ins in the Russian. Intervals between the ranks were one pace for the British, 13ins for the French and 14ins for the Russians. This dense mass of men could deliver a heavy fire, but its very density equally made it an excellent target (especially for artillery). When firing at close range it was even more necessary to aim low; some sources recalled aiming at the enemies' feet so that the kick of the musket would not throw the barrel too high.

(Left) From the moment the first volley was delivered everything to a battalion's front was obscured by the dense, dirty-white smoke produced by black powder. It choked the throat and stung the eyes, and a few volleys on a still day isolated each man from all but his closest comrades. It was only when a man close to him fell and the sergeant shouted Close up! that he could even tell that the enemy were still there and firing. Another disorienting feature of black powder battles was the intense noise. Cannon and massed muskets roaring in such close proximity was terrifying for many a raw recruit, and, together with the smoke, could utterly confuse even an experienced soldier. Conversely, soldiers were encouraged by hearing their own artillery bombarding the enemy. Many memoirs record the author's surviving being hit by spent musket balls; these lost their velocity very quickly, and were seldom deadly at 200 yards.

Relatively few deaths were inflicted with the bayonets of Napoleonic armies. Prolonged mêlées at close quarters (the French slang term loosely translates as "fork suppers") were fairly unusual events except during the storming of fortified positions. Before two opposing infantry lines met in hand-to-hand combat it was usual for one or the other to give way; by the time they reached the critical distance the attackers' evident determination or the defenders' firepower had usually broken the morale of one or the other and decided the outcome.

(Right) The muskets of all armies could be fitted – not very securely – with long socket bayonets which twisted onto the muzzle by means of a right-angled slot; the blades were usually triangular in section. Their main practical value was as a deterrent to horses when infantry were drawn up in tight formation to receive a cavalry attack; and to extend the reach of a foot soldier if he was attacked by a horseman.

(Below) A superb sergeant of French Guard Grenadiers demonstrates bayonet fighting drill.

The British infantry were renowned for awaiting their attackers in silence, often sheltered by the lie of the land until the last moment; then delivering one or two volleys at very short range, before launching an immediate and noisy bayonet charge through the smoke. For example, at Talavera in July 1809 Sherbrooke's 1st Division were given orders to hold fire until the French came within fifty yards, then to fire a single volley and charge. This order was impeccably carried out; though suffering from the enemy's musketry the division held its fire until the French were so close that their leading ranks "went down in swathes". The enemy broke in disorder before the British charge, and fell back over the Portina brook.

On this occasion, unfortunately, "The divisional general had apparently forgotten to caution his colonels against the danger of carrying their advance too far. Instead of contenting themselves with chasing the broken enemy as far as the brook, and then returning to their positions, the four brigades of the first division all crossed the water and pursued the French into their own ground; the German Legion on the left actually began to push them up the lower slopes of the Cerro de Cascajal, while the Guards on the right went forward far into the rolling plain in front of them. Cameron halted his two battalions not far beyond the Portina; but on each side of him the pursuit was pressed with reckless energy, and without any remembrnce of the fact that the enemy had strong reserves."

In consequence half the strength of the 2nd Line Bn KGL (387 men) fell in 20 minutes, and the 5th Bn lost over 100 prisoners. The Foot Guards – 1st Bn/Coldstream and 1st Bn./3rd (Scots) – also suffered heavily: out of their 2,000 men 611 were killed or wounded. It was not only the British cavalry that could become impetuous and charge too far; as Sergeant Anton of the Black Watch remarked, "There is something animating to a soldier in the clash of the fixing bayonet; more particularly so when it is thought that the scabbard is not to receive it until it drinks the blood of its foe."

THE RIFLEMEN

Raised for the British army in 1800, the Experimental Corps of Riflemen were soon to prove themselves and their weapon, the Baker rifle. Taken into the Line as the 95th (Rifle) Regiment of Foot in 1802, they became an élite unit of Wellington's army in the Peninsular and Waterloo campaigns.

The need for skillful skirmishers armed with a weapon of much greater accurate range than the redcoats' smoothbore "Brown Bess" had been acknowledged for a generation. During the American War of Independence in the late 1770s the British army had made considerable use of light infantry tactics, and had employed some German riflemen ("Jägers"), while the long-range sniping of American riflemen had become notorious. Rifles – weapons with spiral grooves cut down the inside of the bore – put a spin on the ball as it was fired, making them accurate to about 300 yards. Their drawbacks were that they were slower to load; and that to take advantage of their range men had to be trained to a high standard in individual marksmanship and the skills of individual fieldcraft.

Colonel Coote Manningham (41st Foot) and Lieutenant-Colonel William Stewart (67th) submitted a paper to the military authorities pointing out the need for a regiment in the British army furnished with such weapons and trained in such skills. This met with a favourable reception, and a circular dated 17 January 1800 was sent by order of the Commander-in-Chief, the Duke of York, to the 2nd Bn The Royals, the 21st, 23rd, 25th, 27th, 29th, 49th, 55th, 69th, 71st, 72nd, 79th, 85th and 92nd Foot. Each regiment was to select two sergeants, two corporals and 30 men, "such as appear most capable of receiving the above instructions, and most competent to the performance of the duty of riflemen." A single captain, lieutenant and ensign were also to be sent by each regiment so that the best of them could be selected for what was obviously to be an élite formation. Eight drummers were also required to act as buglers.

Some of these regiments were conscientious, including – unsurprisingly – the 92nd (Gordon Highlanders), who were informed by regimental order of 24 February 1800 that "The Major expects that the detachment will conduct itself in such a manner as to do credit to the regiment … Ensign Cameron will so exert himself on the march, and after he has arrived at Horsham, that his detachment will

appear as respectable in the corps they are to join as the Regiment has always done … ". Human nature being what it is, some other colonels took the opportunity to rid themselves of their most undesirable elements; an order of 22 March instructs six of the regiments to replace 52 unsuitable men.

To complete the strength of the Corps the authorities called upon 33 of the Fencible Regiments (a class of militia) serving in Ireland each to provide 12 active young men as volunteers at a bounty of ten guineas each; and the same terms were offered to volunteers from the Scottish Fencibles. Indeed, so many early recruits were Scottish that in its early days a distinct Highland company existed within the Rifle Corps (Kincaid mentions this company as late as 1812 in the storming of the breach at Ciudad Rodrigo). Recruiting parties also visited Manchester, Nottingham, Berwick, Edinburgh and Glasgow, soliciting enlistment in what was supposedly a privileged new unit armed with a miraculous weapon.

Coote Manningham was the regiment's colonel, with William Stewart as his lieutenant-colonel; between them they were to forge their riflemen into a deadly efficient fighting force. Stewart's detailed standing orders, the Regulations for the Rifle Corps formed at Blatchinton Barracks under the command of Colonel Manningham, August 15th 1800, were published in 1801.

Until now the British infantry had depended upon unthinking obedience to orders so as to bring their massed, simultaneous fire to bear upon the enemy. It had been understood since the French-Indian War of the 1750s in America that light infantry sharpshooters were of great value in support of the Line; but such units had tended to be gathered for the length of a campaign and then dispersed. Pressure for the permanent institution of light infantry was now gathering momentum, and from 1803 this movement would see the 43rd and 52nd Foot being specially trained in these skills alongside the Rifle Corps at Shorncliffe, Kent, under overall command of the innovative Sir John Moore.

The core of the new training was to instil the initiative and tactical flexibility which open order tactics demanded. In the new regulations we find: "In a Regiment of Riflemen each company must be formed upon the principle of being separate from and totally independent of another." On campaign the companies would often be dispersed to

act independently; their captains would enjoy considerable freedom of decision, and "were encouraged to carry out their duties as Company Commanders without waiting for directions and orders upon every conceivable subject." Officers were to be permanently allocated to companies to build esprit de corps; each company was divided into four equal parts, with an even spread of officers and NCOs, so that even platoons and half-platoons could act independently if required. "In every half-platoon one soldier of merit will be selected and upon him the charge of a squad devolves in the absence of both the officers and non-commissioned officers from it. As from among these four chosen men all corporals are to be appointed, the best men are alone to be selected for this distinction."

Equally significant for the fighting style of the unit was the order that "Every Corporal, Private and Bugler will select a comrade of the rank differing from his own, i.e. front and rear rank, and is never to change him without permission of his Captain. Comrades are always to have the same berth in quarters; and that they may be as little separate as possible in either barracks or the field, will form the same file on parade and go on the same duties with arms … The Corporal's comrade should either be the chosen man or some steady man of the squad who can occasionally help him in his duty … ".

This wholly new approach to the management of the common soldier was underlined by provision in the regulations for the reward of individual behaviour with regimental medals for good conduct and acts of valour in the field. Riflemen were divided into classes according to their results at target practice, the better shots receiving marksmen's distinctions. A regimental library and school were also proposed, and athletic exercises were to be encouraged. All these innovations were designed to create an ideal of individual efficiency and self-respect within the regiment; and the battle record of the 95th was to prove the soundness of the new system.

A committee of field officers was ordered to assemble at Woolwich on 1 February 1800 to select a rifle for the use of the new corps. Weapons from America, France, Germany, Holland and Spain as well as Britain were examined; but it was that made by Ezekiel Baker, based upon the well-established German Jäger pattern, which was chosen after trials. His barrel was 2ft 6ins long, with seven grooves and rifled one quarter turn. When Baker demonstrated his weapon he scored 32 hits out of 34 on a human-sized target at 100 yards, and 22 out of 24 hits at 200 yards. In 1805, 1,663 rifles were produced and in 1806 the number rose to 3,379. At first the calibre was .70in, but this was soon reduced to .62in or "carbine bore".

(Left) The Riflemen were soon set apart from the Line by their uniforms. The clothing warrant of 20 May 1801 allowed annually for each sergeant, corporal, drummer and private man: "A green coat without lace – A kersey waistcoat – A cap, cockade and tuft as specified (viz., a cap made of felt and leather with brass plates cockade and tuft conformable to a pattern approved by us, the felt crown of the cap and tuft to be supplied annually, the leather part and brass plate and the leather cockade every two years) – A pair of green pantaloons." The green uniform (faced for the 95th with black, piped white) and the buglehorn badge were both traditional elements of German Jäger dress. NCOs wore white sleeve chevrons and sergeants scarlet sashes with a black line. Leather equipment was black, and included a waistbelt supporting a pouch for loose bullets and a bayonet, and a crossbelt supporting a cartridge pouch with a powder horn strung over it.

The greatest accuracy was obtained by loading with a ball wrapped in a greased cloth patch (held in a butt-trap in the rifle stock), and loose powder from the flask. Rifleman William Green recorded carrying both 50 rounds of paper cartridge and 30 loose balls, and cartridges must presumably have been used in relatively close-quarter battle when speed was more important than exact accuracy. Forcing the tight-fitting ball down the rifled barrel was a slow task, and Baker wrote that "When the 95th Regiment was raised by Government, which is now called the rifle brigade, I supplied them with a few hundreds of small wooden mallets to drive in the ball, but they found them very inconvenient and very soon dispensed with them. The loading is performed equally well without them." When the 5th Bn, 60th Regiment received the Baker in 1808 their commanding officer also applied for 450 mallets; he later requested powder flasks "of the same description as those of the 95th Regiment."

While a veteran with a smoothbore musket might load and fire three rounds a minute, modern trials show that a rifleman might have difficulty achieving a sustained rate of more than one. When the barrel became fouled by repeated firing his rate slowed; but loose ball could be loaded unpatched down the constricted bore, giving less accuracy but at least keeping the weapon in action. Lacking the rifling grooves, smoothbores were easier to clean temporarily by scraping with the ramrod and/or urinating down the barrel.

(Probably the oddest load a Baker ever fired was due to the frustration of one Private Brotherwood, "always a lively fellow, but rather irritable in disposition. Just as the French went to the right-about, I remember he damned them furiously; and all his bullets being gone, he grabbed a razor from his haversack, rammed it down, and fired it after them.")

Originally fitted with a 17in triangular bayonet fixed by a spring, the Baker was later given a flat-bladed sword bayonet, which at 24ins gave the rifleman (whose weapon was shorter than a musket) an equal reach. The fact that when attached to the muzzle - bar provided the sword bayonet effectively prevented the massively unbalanced rifle from being fired meant that it was a weapon of last resort for desperate situations only. Although probably used more for camp chores or as a hand weapon than in its fixed position, it is remembered to this day in the traditional use of the term "sword" instead of bayonet by the Royal Green Jackets.

(Right) The Rifles enjoyed a social cachet as a military élite from the earliest years, and this was emphasised by the officers' uniform, which had a strong light cavalry flavour. The jacket, with its three rows of ball buttons and lavish cord braiding, resembled a light cavalry dolman; and some officers even wore a fur-trimmed pelisse overjacket slung from one shoulder.

The Hanoverian soldiers of the King's German Legion were among the best troops in Wellington's army. This powerful volunteer corps provided eight Line battalions, light and heavy cavalry and artillery; but the first units to be formed in 1805 were two Light Battalions. Uniformed much like the British 95th, they gave distinguished service for ten years, right up to the heroic stand of Baring's 2nd Light Bn KGL at La Haye Sainte on the field of Waterloo.

All skirmishers operated in pairs, one attempting to remain loaded at all times. The great Prussian commander General Yorck defined a rifleman thus: "The rifle was not made for drill, and drilling is not the Jäger's purpose ... It is an irrevocable basic rule that the Jäger never hurries his fire, but always shoots with effect. It is an equally irrevocable rule that two Jäger always defend one another, that is, always act in groups of two – front and rear men. These two Jäger must at all times consider themselves as one body; one defends the other, so that when one man has fired and is therefore defenceless, the other has loaded

and is capable of defensive action. This rule must be an unbreakable law to every Jäger, since his honour and life depend on it."

We have a vivid account of what it was like to fight in a Rifles skirmish line:

"Taking advantage of whatever cover I could find, I threw myself down behind a small bank, where I lay so secure that, although the Frenchmen's bullets fell pretty thickly around, I was enabled to knock several over without being dislodged; in fact, I fired away every round I had in my pouch whilst lying in this spot. Joseph Cochan was by my side loading and firing very industriously about this period of the day. Thirsting with heat and action he lifted his canteen to his mouth; 'Here's to you, old boy' he said, as he took a pull at its contents. As he did so a bullet went through the canteen, and perforating his brain, killed him in a moment. Another man fell close to him almost immediately, struck by a ball in the thigh. I saw a man named Symmonds struck full in the face by a round shot, and he came to the ground a headless trunk."

(Below & opposite) The 95th Rifles skirmishing; the extra accuracy of the Baker rifle – note the simple rear sights provided – could be exploited by careful resting and aiming. The Rifles were trained to shoot from a variety of supported positions; this Chosen Man, his status marked by the white band around his sleeve, is using his ramrod braced between rifle and belt to steady his aim. The smartness of his uniform suggests that he is at the start of a campaign; John Harris decribed the appearance of the 2nd Bn when they finally reached England after the retreat to Corunna in 1809:

"Our poor bare feet once more touched English ground. The inhabitants flocked down to the beach to see us as we did so, and they must have been a good deal surprised at the spectacle we presented. Our beards were long and ragged; almost all were without shoes and stockings; many had their clothes and accoutrements in fragments, with their heads swathed in old rags, and our weapons were covered with rust; whilst not a few had now, from toil and fatigue, become quite blind."

(Right) The shako gave enough support for the muzzle when firing prone. Note the line of the top of the rifle stock, straighter than that of a musket in order to bring the marksman's eye easily in line with the barrel; and the cheek piece on the inside of the butt. Useful targets were enemy artillery batteries, which before the introduction of the Baker could outrange anything the helpless infantry could fire back at them. Riflemen could silence them by sniping from concealed forward positions, picking off the crews and horses one by one.

(Right) Rifleman Tom Plunkett used this back prone position (but with one leg cocked back to tension the rifle sling) at Cacabelos in the Peninsula. His target was the dashing young French General Colbert, whom he shot through the head. William Surtees recalled: "The force of the enemy greatly exceeded ours, yet our people drove them back with great loss, killing General Colbert, who commanded the advance. This was done by a noted pickle of the name of Tom Plunkett, who, fearless of all danger to himself, got sufficiently nigh to make sure of his mark, and shot him, which with the fire of the others, caused great havoc in the enemy's ranks, and sent them flying to the rear much faster than they advanced." Not everyone approved of Plunkett's killing the French general, regarding it as no better than assassination:

"… his fine martial figure, his voice, his gestures, and, above all, his great valour, had excited the admiration of the British, and a general feeling of sorrow was predominant when the gallant soldier fell." (Napier, Volume 1)

GALLOPING AT EVERYTHING

Our cavalry captured many colours and prisoners, among the latter Prince Repnin, Commander of the Noble Guard. This regiment, composed of the most brilliant of the young Russian nobility, lost heavily, because the swagger in which they had indulged against the French having come to the ears of our soldiers, these, and above all, the Grenadiers à Cheval attacked them with fury, shouting as they passed their great sabres through their bodies: 'We will give the ladies of St. Petersburg something to cry about!' (Marbot)

Where are our cavalry? Why don't they come and pitch into those French fellows? (British infantry officer in square at Waterloo, charged by French cavalry)

(Below) In all period armies there were several orders of dress; this is a French heavy cavalryman of the Grenadiers à Cheval de la Garde *wearing a short, plain stable jacket and fatigue trousers with a* bonnet de police *in regimental colours. Stable jackets were worn for foot drill and barracks dress, and not always when working with the horses, when shirt-sleeve order or work smocks might be more appropriate due to the malodor-* *ous substances produced by horses … This private soldier ("trooper" was not a period term) is picking gravel and compacted dirt out of his mount's hoof – a constantly necessary chore, especially on the march, if he did not want his horse lamed and himself left to straggle after the column on foot.*

(Opposite) Lancer of a French Line regiment, seen from the perspective of an unlucky infantryman.

Napoleonic cavalry was divided into three classes: light, medium and heavy. Light cavalry such as the French Chasseurs à Cheval, British Light Dragoons and Hussars all (despite the pretensions of certain hussar regiments) performed similar duties. These were primarily scouting, screening and raiding, but included a full-blooded charging role on the battlefield when necessary. The light cavalry provided piquets and outposts, generally being the first element of the army in contact with the enemy, at least in daytime – at nightfall they could be withdrawn and replaced by infantry, depending upon terrain and circumstances.

Another form of light cavalry were the Lancers found in Polish, French, Austrian, Prussian and Russian armies of the period. Designated as light troops, they nonetheless recruited taller and more powerfully built men whenever possible, as the lance was a heavy weapon to wield effectively. When, by a decree of 18 June 1811, Napoleon formed his own nine Line lancer units he did so mainly by converting existing Dragoon regiments (1st, 3rd, 8th, 9th, 10th and 29th), adding the Polish 1st and 2nd Vistula Lancers and the 30th Chasseurs à Cheval. Their personnel, horses and indeed uniform and equipment differed very little from that of the remaining dragoon regiments, so it can be argued that the lancer should be classed as a medium cavalryman.

After the mauling the British infantry received at Albuera in May 1811 at the hands of the Vistula Lancers, it was decided to experiment with lances in the British cavalry, and troops of both the 12th and 15th Light Dragoons conducted exercises with the lance. Colonel Stewart of the 12th reported that "Good swordsmen have no reason to fear the lance if they are equally good horsemen", and it was generally felt that no significant advantage could be gained by the lance's introduction. (This decision was reversed shortly after the Napoleonic Wars, when the 9th, 12th, 16th and 19th Light Dragoons were transformed into Lancer regiments during 1816-17; the 19th were disbanded and the 17th Light Dragoons took their place in 1821.)

Dragoons were classed as either Light or Heavy in the British army; but a French dragoon weighed in at around the same as a British heavy or Household cavalryman as far as riding weight in the saddle was concerned. The real difference lay in the weight and quality of their respective mounts. In the French service there was still an echo of the dragoon's original identity as a mere mounted infantryman, given any old hack to ride on the march but fighting on foot; and at various times they still formed dismounted regiments at need. In Britain this historical association had long since faded away, and dragoons were simply light or heavy cavalry, provided with good horses. French dragoons were thus classed as medium cavalry, and performed outpost duties, a role not usually undertaken by the British heavies.

The true heavy cavalry were the Cuirassiers, not all of whom still actually wore the full back-and-breast armour, e.g. the Prussians, who discarded it before 1800. These Prussian heavy units were mounted on big, good quality horses of the Holstein and Oldenburg breeds. After the French victories over

(*Below & right*) *Frederick the Great of Prussia raised the 5th or Black Hussars in 1741; they were also nicknamed the Death Hussars from their cap plate. After a distinguished battle history, they became in 1808 the* Leib *or lifeguard Hussars. In Prussia's 1806-07 campaigns against Napoleon they fought at Eylau and Heilsberg, where they destroyed the French 55th Line regiment and captured its eagle; the regimental officers were awarded the Pour le Merite for outstanding valour. On 29 December 1808 the regiment was split into two, the 1st and 2nd Life Hussars. After Prussia fell under French domination two squadrons from each formed the 1st Combined Hussars in the Prussian contingent of Napoleon's Grande Armée of 1812. They served in Macdonald's X Corps,* and one of the first crosses of the Légion d'Honneur awarded in Russia was won by Lieutenant von Raven at the Dvina river crossings in July 1812.

When Prussia rose against Napoleon in 1813 the Life regiments fought in many actions as part of Blücher's Silesian Army, including Gross Gorschen (2 May), Bautzen (20-21 May), Rochlitz (17 August), where they charged an enemy battery and captured two guns, and Wartenburg (3 October), where they overran another six cannon. For the decisive battle of Leipzig (16-19 October) they were brigaded with the 3rd Brandenburg Hussars north-west of the city; the brigade broke Marmont's cavalry, taking two colours and six guns. At Freiburg two days later they liberated 4,000 prisoners.

By December 1813 the 2nd Life Hussars were on the Rhine, but broken down by this relentless campaigning; their uniforms were threadbare and their equipment and saddlery in little better order. Grey uniforms were supplied by Britain to help their refit; and so was this 1796 Le Marchant light cavalry sabre, copied locally as the so-called "Blücher" sabre. Production in Prussia was quite extensive; when withdrawn from the Line regiments they were reissued to the Landwehr, and continued in service well after the Franco-Prussian War of 1870-71 - they were even used by German depot regiments in the First World War.

Until 1808, 16-20 men per squadron carried rifles. After 1808 this was increased to 48, the remaining men carrying the short cavalry carbine and officers, NCOs and trumpeters two pistols each.

Prussia in 1806 as many of these as possible were appropriated into the French army (although they often proved too much horse for the French riders to handle!) To save on the weight carried the Austrians came up with the idea of issuing a breast plate alone and dispensing with the back plate. While this undoubtedly saved wear on a horse's back, it left their cuirassiers only partly protected in a swirling fight – the left kidney area was a favoured target for a pursuer, especially a lancer.

It is, of course, for the full-blooded charge, flat out at the gallop, that the cavalry were renowned. Examples abound, such as Murat's mass charge with 80 squadrons, formed in a brigade column and hurled by the Emperor into the Russian centre at Eylau in 1807. In this charge the formidable Grenadiers à Cheval broke completely through the enemy and found themselves stranded behind the Russian lines. With typical panache Colonel Lepic halted his "Black Horses", reformed and realigned them, then charged back through the way he had come in.

At Waterloo, William Ponsonby's Union Brigade of three heavy Dragoon regiments caused havoc amongst General d'Erlon's I Corps when they crossed the hedges that the Allies were defending and charged through the French infantry, capturing the regimental eagles of the 45th and 105th Line regiments. Throwing back the French attack, they did not halt and rally, but – typically of British cavalry – continued right into the French batteries, sabreing gunners and limber horses. They were finally counter-attacked by lancers and cuirassiers and bloodily pursued back to their own lines, with huge losses. That any got back at all was due to the simultaneous charge of

If infantry were well closed up in square formation, not too badly mauled by artillery, and kept their nerve, then charging cavalry were easy enough for them to handle. Caught out in the open, however, a straggler from the column of march, a skirmisher (like this Light Company man of the 1st Foot Guards), or individual soldiers fleeing from a broken formation would stand little chance against formed cavalry. The rider's speed allowed him to overtake infantry with ease; his height gave him a long reach, and the sheer size and weight of the horse gave a huge advantage. Simple terror also played a part: when an

infantryman found himself caught in the open by cavalry he knew what his fate was likely to be. Such encounters were usually one-sided – but not always:

"A lancer made several lunges at Dooley, who was wounded in the arm and being exasperated he sprang out of the ranks and chased the lancer; the latter returned at full tilt, Dooley faced his antagonist in the open. Everybody expected to see Dooley spitted like a hog, however, he dextrously caught the lance on his bayonet and threw the point clear of himself and the next moment the lancer was on the ground, pierced through the body."

the heavy Household Brigade, which overthrew the French cuirassiers positioned by Napoleon to counter any such attack by the British cavalry. The results of this wild charge cannot be denied, however: d'Erlons corps was broken, and many of the French guns were not brought back into action for hours.

It was hardly surprising that the cavalry, with their long aristocratic traditions, elaborate uniforms and glory-grabbing engagements, were seen as the most glamorous arm of the service. But, as they say, "There are old cavalrymen, and bold cavalrymen; but no old, bold cavalrymen." Take as an example

(Left & below) The first lance-armed unit in Napoleon's cavalry was a regiment of Polish volunteers – Poland, long defeated and partitioned by her neighbours, looked to France to restore her independence, and provided the Emperor with many of his finest foreign troops. The Lancers of the Vistula Legion served in Spain; and at Albuera on 16 May 1811, under cover of a rainstorm, they caught General Colborne's brigade of British infantry stretched out in line formation rather than in squares for all-round defence. When the action was over the 1/3rd Buffs, the 2/48th Northamptons and the 2/66th Berkshires had been reduced from 1,651 officers and men to just 597 unwounded of all ranks, commanded by a French Royalist emigré captain.

Regiments charged in two successive ranks, and at first both ranks were equipped with lances; but this could be as dangerous to their own first rank as it was to the enemy – when a second rank arrived to reinforce a first wave already involved in a mêlée, many an unlucky soldier found himself spitted on a comrade's lance. The French later removed the lance from the rear rankers, henceforth armed with sabre, carbine and pistol like the rest of the light horse.

This rear rank man of the 1st Vistula Lancers wears the Polish style of uniform which would become typical for this type of troops in many armies: a square-topped czapka headgear and a short-tailed kurtka jacket with a buttoned-back plastron front and piping on the rear seams. He has his cloak slung around his body over the right shoulder, protecting his chest and left kidney – this was designated in both sword and lance training as a good target when in pursuit of an enemy. The order for the regiment to "roll cloaks" was a clear sign to the men that combat was imminent.

The Poles had a merciless reputation. Major Brooke, captured at Albuera while in command of the 2/48th, was being escorted to the rear by two French infantrymen when a lancer rode up and cut him down, then made his horse trample over him, leaving Brooke for dead.

(Opposite) A cavalry officer at his ease; the long "flame" of the bonnet is folded and tucked into the side of the "turban" and the tassel on the end of it is brought forward to hang at the front. Unless they were on a formal parade such details as the colour of a waistcoat were a matter for individual officers.

General Antoine Lasalle, *beau sabreur* of the French light cavalry, leader in 1806 of *la brigade infernale* (the "hellish brigade" of hussars), a devil with women, and dead at the age of 32 – shot between the eyes on the field of Wagram in 1809 on the last charge of the day. Or the British General Le Marchant, whose charge at the head of the British heavy cavalry at Salamanca in 1812 cost him his life. His brigade smashed the left wing of the French army, and retained its discipline in a manner previously unseen for the British cavalry. Le Marchant himself was an expert swordsman and horseman, having written the 1796 *Sword Exercise* and designed new swords for both the light and heavy cavalry. At Salamanca he was seen to cut down six men with his own hand before a bullet ripped through his sash, breaking his spine and pitching him face down dead on the field of battle.

Life for a cavalryman, be he general or private soldier, could be just as dangerous as that in any other arm of the service.

THE HORSES

In theory, five years was the minimum age for a cavalry mount in the French army, although in practice younger horses were taken as the wastage of repeated campaigns made the problem of providing remounts increasingly serious. The nadir was reached in 1813 after the appalling losses of the Russian campaign, when the army had just 15,000 largely untrained horses of which only about 3,000 were judged suitable and ready for cavalry service.

Napoleon's attitude to horseflesh was as coldly practical as it was to manpower: "(Cavalry) should not be handled with any miserly instinct to keep it intact ... I do not wish the horses to be spared if they catch men ... Take no heed of the complaints of the cavalry, for if such great objects may be obtained as the destruction of a whole enemy army, the state can afford

to lose a few hundred horses from exhaustion ... "

The day to day duty of maintaining the cavalry's mounts in the field fell to the regimental farriers; only at a farrier's request would a horse be examined by the regiment's single veterinary. Although these latter were graduates of the Écoles Hippiatriques at Alfort or Lyon, they could not attain a higher rank than sergeant. Period veterinary practice included the bleeding of sick animals; and the collecting together of any debilitated animals for care – which had the effect of spreading contagion among animals many of whom might only be suffering initially from some relatively minor complaint.

It was the sergeant-farrier's job to inspect the condition of the horses at each of the three daily grooming parades, or at each of the prescribed halts on the march to rest the horses and re-adjust girths, sursingles and other tack. The farriers, who shoed the horses, also rode at the tail of the troops to pick up any horseshoes which might be cast on the march.

In 1791 the London Veterinary College was founded, and it was from this establishment that veterinary surgeons were recruited for the British army thereafter. Before 1791 regimental farriers were in charge of horse care, and its quality therefore varied greatly between individual squadrons, let alone on a regimental basis. Farriers lacked any uniform training or education, relying upon traditional remedies and methods. Many beasts became lame due to bad shoeing, and had to be destroyed. During the retreat to Waal in the severe winter of 1794 the British expedition to Flanders lost far more horses to indifferent horse care than to enemy action, a fact duly noted by the Army Reform Committee. One defect was the lack of snow shoes and frost nails for the cavalry. Napoleon's cavalry were also to struggle through the retreat from Moscow in 1812 without the necessary shoes and nails to enable them to move over ice and frozen snow; only the Imperial household carried supplies of these essentials. In this the French army had no excuse, as their own veterinary services had been established long before their British counterparts.

Initially the first year's syllabus at the London Veterinary College included anatomy, conformation, physiology and external diseases; the second year, *materia medica* and medical botany; the third and final year, epizootic diseases, pathology, hospital practice and, last but not least, shoeing. However, by 1795 the cavalry's need for veterinary surgeons resulted in the training for army vets being reduced to a six-month crash course.

The standard of British army horse care was gradually raised, partly by the example of such progressive practicioners as John Shipp. Many farriers resented the intrusion of the veterinarians, but slowly the new methods filtered down through the ranks. Veterinary surgeons liased with the senior farrier, known as the "farrier major" and having the rank of staff sergeant, as did the armourer and saddler; assistant farriers ranked only as privates. Daily feeding and management of the horses was supervised by the quartermaster, who was also required to refer horses for shoeing.

That well thought-of animal the "cavalry black" (this being a generic term, not referring only to colour) had been largely replaced in the British army by the early 19th century with lighter hunter-type animals, selective breeding producing faster horses for domestic as well as military purposes. Sir Walter Gilbey gave the following average heights for English thoroughbreds: 1700, 14 hands; 1800, 14.3 hands; 1900, 15.2

(Opposite) Reconstructions of French 1786 model cavalry carbine, and a pair of 1777 pattern pistols. A cavalryman who was issued with two pistols was indeed fortunate; regardless of the regulation scale of issue there were seldom enough to go round, and a number of elderly and foreign types were to be seen throughout the period. Trumpeters and NCOs were more likely to receive the pair; but even if you had only one, it at least left the right hand pistol holster free for carrying your horse grooming kit.

(Opposite below) The holsters were slung at the saddle pommel, with the pistols butt forward and usually covered by the sheepskin. This made them awkward to draw in a hurry.

(Above) Heavy cavalry preferred straight or almost straight blades; the French, like this Horse Grenadier of the Guard, were taught that it was better to strike with the point and press home their marked advantage of greater weight, which could be better transmitted through a straight blade. Le Marchant designed a new British heavy cavalry blade in 1796 based upon Austrian examples he had seen in the Low Countries; however, the drill he devised still employed the classic six cuts. "Consequently, out of every 20 blows aimed by them, 19 missed. But if the edge of the blade found its mark only once it was a terrible blow, and it was not unusual to see an arm cut clean from the body" (Charles Parquin).

(Right) Hilt of a straight Dragoon sabre of Year XII pattern under the Revolutionary calendar (September 1803 - September 1804).

hands. One hand equals 4ins, and horses are measured from the bottom of the hoof when the leg is upright to the top of the wither. In today's terms any horse under 14.2 hands is considered a pony, good-sized hunters being in the 16 hands and upwards bracket. These new hunter-type horses fell into light, medium or heavy categories and could thus be employed by the various weights of cavalry. Wellington himself kept seven chargers and eight hunters, even having his own pack of hounds in the Peninsula. A charger is generally thought of as better looking and perhaps larger than a hunter. However, Wellington's favourite mount Copenhagen was a chestnut ex-racehorse with speed and endurance, but standing only 15 hands high.

The colonel of the 12th Light Dragoons in 1811 described the type of horse required for the light cavalry as: "Active and fully master of 17 stone. Remember stout and good limbs – stout backs – good feet – open in the counter – good shoulders and well up before. Deep chested and not lightly carcassed, not too heavy in the hind quarters, but strong in the gammon and open between the jaw."

Most of the many horses required to mount the British light cavalry were bought in Britain, as the local breeds available on campaign proved unsuitable. The 20th Light Dragoons were despatched to Portugal in 1808 without mounts but obtaining suitable indigenous beasts proved very difficult, and the experiment was not repeated. Given a choice, officers purchasing remounts would buy horses of between five and six years of age for between £40 and £45; but often there were not enough

suitable horses available in that age bracket at a reasonable price. As the horse's age increased its price dropped, giving rise to older horses on home service being sent on campaign and replaced on home service by the younger, more expensive animals, these younger remounts requiring more training. Naturally the Staff rode more expensive horses in the charger mould, and these could cost up to £75.

Wellington wrote in 1813: "A Dragoon's horse costs 25 guineas, rising 3 and not fit for work or service for 1½ to 2 years. We prefer them here at 5 years so it is not unreasonable to add to the sum about half as much again. Would it be extravagant to give £45 or 40 guineas for 5 or 6 year old horses and mares for regiments on service and £45 or guineas for horses for artillery abroad? If not we must draft the 5 and 6 year olds from regiments at home and make a great effort to replace them by 2 and 3 year olds at the usual price. Old and worn horses if sent out are useless."

BRITISH ORGANISATION AND TACTICS

Each British cavalry regiment was organised in a number of squadrons, a squadron being further subdivided into two troops, the right and left.

When the war began against Revolutionary France the cavalry regiments' establishment was increased from six to nine troops until the 1794 campaign, when the cavalry reverted to the six-troop regiment (except for the 1st Dragoon Guards). Two troops of each regiment remained at the regimental

(Above) The short-barrelled, smooth-bore flintlock saddle pistol was of very little value as a battlefield weapon unless it was fired at point blank range. Modern tests achieved only an 18in group when ten shots were fired – from a steady rested aim, not the back of an excited horse – at 15 yards. It is easy to see why so many contemporary writers dismissed it as useful only for dispatching wounded horses, unless the muzzle was virtually touching the opponent's body. This soldier of the Élite Company of the French 7th Hussars lets his sabre hang by its fist strap as he aims and fires; note that he holds the pistol on its side, with the priming pan immediately above the touch hole, in hopes of a more certain ignition.

(Opposite) Cavalry carbines were a little better than pistols; and General de Brack, whose light cavalry manual became a standard work, reckoned them to be of use out to 90 metres. Other diarists appear to disagree; and given the inaccuracy of the much longer-barrelled infantry musket at that range, one must conclude that if he was telling the truth then de Brack's Red Lancers of the Guard were remarkable shots.

The carbine was typically carried from a crossbelt which also supported its cartridge pouch; a sprung, swivelling "dog-lead" clip engaged with an iron ring running free on a rail on the left side of the stock, allowing the carbine to be brought up to the shoulder without unclipping it.

depot on home service. In 1800 regiments were raised to ten troops, two still remaining at the depot; the 1811 reorganisation reduced this to eight troops for the heavy units, with two still forming the depot; light regiments remained at ten troops. By the end of 1813 light cavalry regiments were increased to 12 troops; however, most regiments on active service were lucky if they could field 400 sabres.

The troop was the smallest tactical unit for field manoeuvre but smaller detachments were used for piquet duty and reconnaissance patrols. In the Peninsula British light cavalry regiments at first found it difficult to master outpost duties; it took them a long time to match the efficient King's German Legion in these tasks.

British light cavalry regiments were raised in the mid-18th century without any standard guidelines as to their role in the army. In 1776 Thomas Sime's work *The Military Guide for Young Officers* included advice on the role of the light cavalry, stating that as well as reconnaissance, "Light cavalry are also to be made use of for distant advanced posts, to prevent the army from being falsely alarmed or surprised by the enemy. Parties are also to be sent out to distress the enemy, by depriving them of forage and provisions; by surprising their convoys, attacking their baggage, harassing them on their march, cutting off small detachments, and sometimes carrying off foraging parties; in short, of seizing all opportunities to do them as much damage as they possibly can.

"Light cavalry are moreover to be employed in raising contributions: and when the army marches they may compose the advance guard; reconnoitring the front and flanks carefully,

and sending intelligence to the Commander in Chief with expedition whenever they discover the enemy, or any kind of danger: and, when other troops cannot be spared, they may form the rear guard or cover the baggage."

In 1778 Captain Hinde published his *Discipline of the Light Horse*, in which he outlined training, armament and development. But while it is one thing to issue training manuals, it is quite another to ensure that they are used; and many regiments continued training for the one thing that they desired – the full regimental charge. This attitude was not helped by the success of a light cavalry charge at Villers en Cauchies on 24 April 1794. The 15th Light Dragoons were the "culprits", in conjunction with two squadrons of Austrian hussars. Two of the 15th's squadrons, along with the Austrians, broke through six battalions of French infantry at only light cost to themselves. The other light cavalry regiments looked on with envy, as indeed did many of their heavier brethren.

Major-General David Dundas, the author of an infantry drill manual, witnessed at first hand the poor showing of the cavalry in the Flanders campaign. In June 1795 his work, *Rules and Regulations for the Cavalry*, was ordered by the King to be issued by the Adjutant-General to all cavalry regiments, both light and heavy. Yet another manual appeared in 1796, Major John Gaspard Le Marchant's *Rules and Regulations for the Sword Exercises of the Cavalry*. Based upon the new light and heavy cavalry swords designed by Le Marchant himself, it gave the light cavalry its first uniform set of sword exercises and, incidentally, its first uniform sword; previously each regimental colonel bought whatever style of sword he pleased. Le

(Left) *Officer of the British 15th Hussars, among the first Light Dragoon units to be retitled as Hussars in 1805. At first their headgear was a tall fur busby or colpack, but from 1812 they wore this more practical shako, its scarlet cover being a regimental peculiarity of the 15th. Their uniform appears to be based upon the items sent to the Prince of Wales by his brother the Duke of York from Berlin in 1791; the Prince had requested uniforms, saddles, bridles and complete accoutrements of one of General Zieten's Hussars, along with similar appointments of a hussar officer. Another important contributor was Baron von Linsingen, whose King's German Legion Hussars provided another role model. Eventually the 7th, 10th, 15th and 18th Light Dragoons were all converted to hussar dress; their function was unchanged, however, and their horse sizes were similar to those of light dragoons. The inspection report for the 10th Hussars in 1813 gives their 299 horses as the following heights: 4 at 16 hands, 74 at 15½ , 138 at 15 and 83 at 14½.*

Marchant's manual emphasised the cut rather than the point as used by the French cavalry. While serving with the 16th Light Dragoons he had seen the awful swordsmanship and horsemanship of the British cavalry, and this was his attempt to improve matters, along with the introduction of officer training schools.

British cavalry was eventually to develop an enviable record for horse care and training, but for now it continued to amble along with half-trained horses and men, some regiments being far better than others. Wellington was to comment, "In Spain the Germans, the 14th Light Dragoons, and perhaps the 12th under Fred Ponsonby, were the only regiments that knew their duty and did not get into scrapes of every description." Lieutenant-Colonel Ponsonby prepared the following orders to be read to the 12th Light Dragoons, based upon Von Arentschildt's *Instructions for Cavalry on Outpost Duty*:

"The Commanding Officer desires that the following instructions may be read on three parades by the officers commanding troops when every officer, non-commissioned officer and private is present. As the Regiment is likely to be on outpost duty it is Colonel Ponsonby's wish that the following Regulations should be considered as the standing orders of the Regiment on the subject.

"Officers and non-commissioned officers in command of piquets or patrols are to be particularly careful in sending in reports of the enemies' movements, nothing can be so disgraceful as a dragoon galloping in with a false report of the enemy's advance, the patrol or piquet must himself ascertain the truth and then have it conveyed as rapidly as he thinks the circumstances require to the commanding officer in the rear. All reports must be made in writing except when the enemy

is advancing so rapidly that no time is to be spared.

"Officers or non-commissioned officers on patrol must never halt to feed in a town and whenever they do halt, which should be in an open place, a vidette must be placed.

"A flag of truce is known by a person coming forward waving his handkerchief or pulling off his hat, or more frequently by a trumpet or drum. The vidette is not to permit him to pass, but is to make a signal by circling his horse. The officer of the piquet is to receive the letters from the flag of truce and give a receipt for them. Non-commissioned officers are to do the same, but no person is to be allowed to pass the vidette without further instructions from the officer commanding the outposts.

"If any movement of the enemy takes place in front of the vidette, except the relief of the enemy's vidette, he is to circle, the piquet is to turn out, and the commander to ascertain the movement before he reports. If near the enemy the piquets must be on the road and upon all occasions a dismounted man who can see the vidette must be placed to warn the piquet if the vidette makes a signal. Half the piquet must always be bridled. Any officer or non-commissioned officer who suffers his piquet or patrol to be surprised is immediately disgraced.

"Every man knows how fatal drunkenness must be wither on patrol or piquet – there is every temptation that the men must resist; they must recollect that they subject themselves to be tried by a General Court Martial and to be shot if guilty of drunkenness when on duty before the enemy, but he hopes they will consider how much the honour of the Regiment depends on them particularly in this.

"If any prisoners are taken they are to be treated kindly, and men found plundering will be severely punished. All horses taken are the property of the regiment, and if sold the money is divided amongst the whole. No man is to go to the rear without an order from an officer, no man must plead ignorance or the example of any other regiment when the orders of his own regiment are so positive."

It was not until the Peninsular War that the British light cavalry were to be used in large numbers, and even so they were to be outnumbered on most occasions, except for the campaigns of Salamanca (1812) and Vittoria (1813). Sir John Moore had only the 18th Hussars and 3rd Light Dragoons of the King's German Legion with him on his march into Spain in 1808. The 7th, 10th and 15th Hussars joined him in time for the 15th to gain yet more glory at Sahagun, where they broke the French 8th Dragoons and 1st Provisional Chasseurs with another of their spirited charges. This time the enemy thought the British hussars were Spanish cavalry, "who never charge home", and obligingly sat still to meet the charge with carbine fire. The 15th took the ineffective carbine fire in their stride as they overturned their opponents in the pre-dawn gloom. The regimental diary of the 15th takes up the story, probably written by the adjutant, C. Jones:

"Day was just now beginning to dawn, and the Regiment instantly formed open column of divisions and continued to trot on parallel to the enemy in order to bring our right flank as forward as their left, all this time within 80 yards of each other. The enemy finding they could not get away, halted and drew up. The 15th wheeled into line, gave three cheers, shouted *Emsdorf and Victory!* which resounded from one end of the line to the other, the bugles sounded the charge which was one of the finest that could be seen, and in one instant we were upon the enemy who stood the charge in the most gallant manner. Between two and three hundred men immediately rode down and the remainder dispersed in every direction. About 200 took the road to Palencia, we had not time to stop up. The little parties of the enemy were now charged by small parties of the Regiment in all quarters, and the rout of the enemy was complete."

Along with their heavier brethren the light cavalry still found it difficult to rally after a charge, the main reason being that they simply did not want to… . As Wellington summed it up, they had a habit of "galloping at everything." When let loose in a charge these dogs of war were almost impossible to control, which is why Wellington kept them on a tight leash whenever possible. He was never much impressed by his cavalry, and after Waterloo he issued his *Instructions to Officers Commanding Brigades of Cavalry in the Army of Occupation*, which specifies the proper conduct of a charge by heavy cavalry:

"1. A reserve must always be kept, to improve a success or to cover an unsuccessful charge. This reserve should not be less than half the total number of sabres and may occasionally be as much as two thirds of it.

"2. Normally a cavalry force should form in three lines; the first and second lines should not be deployed, the reserve may be in column, but so formed as to be easily changed into line.

"3. The second line should be 400 to 500 yards from the first, the reserve a similar distance from the second line. This is not too great a distance to prevent the rear files from improving an advantage gained by the front line, nor too little to prevent a defeated front line from passing between the intervals of its supports without disordering them.

"4. When, however, cavalry is charging infantry, the second line should be only 200 yards behind the first, the object being that it should be able to deliver its charge without delay against a battalion which has spent its fire against a front line and will not be prepared for the charge, pushed in rapid succession to the first.

"5. When the first line delivers its attack at a gallop, the supports must follow at a walk only, less they be carried forward by the rush and get mingled with the line in front at the outset. For order in the supports must be rigidly kept – they are useless if they have got into confusion when they are wanted to sustain and cover a checked first line."

William Tomkinson (of the 16th Light Dragoons, be it noted) believed that "the heavy cavalry have enough to do to sit their horse and keep in the ranks, without giving their attention to any sudden order. Before the enemy, excepting in charging, I never saw troops go beyond a trot, though in some cases it might be required, and therefore in some movements they should be taught to gallop. These are few, such as moving to a flank in open column of divisions or half squadrons, wheeling into line and charging without a halt. In England I never saw nor heard of cavalry taught to charge, disperse and form, which, if I only taught a regiment one thing, I think it should be that."

(Below) For most of the Napoleonic Wars Britain and France were the only two major powers without lancer regiments, but in June 1811 Napoleon converted one Chasseur and six Dragoon regiments into Lancers of the Line, which with the Vistula regiments gave a total of nine. Their brass helmets and green uniforms closely resembled dragoon dress. For the campaign of 1812 Napoleon added a lancer regiment to each heavy cuirassier division, to provide integral light cavalry support against the swarms of Cossacks which were known to be a feature of the Russian army.

Initially the lancer learnt sword, carbine and lance drill on foot, postponing the extra complications caused by the horse. When mounted exercises began some of the younger remount horses were spooked by the lance pennons. To avoid this they were supposed to be accustomed to the pennons while still at the depots, but this was sometimes overlooked – with spectacular results on campaign, when the horses reared and spun around in the ranks. This was, however, the desired effect on the enemy's horses, and the fluttering pennons did often cause confusion in their formations. Lancers carried more equipment than other cavalry regiments; as well as the lance they were to retain sabre, pistol and carbine, making for quite a juggling act when on campaign. Bayonets were another issue item, but were among the first to be jettisoned. Napoleon believed that to be effective his lancers must be fully armed and capable of a dismounted role, although the regimental colonels preferred to keep their men mounted for shock action. The lance was hard to master and not a universally popular weapon; there are accounts of men piling and burning their lances in the freezing cold of the 1812 retreat.

(*Left*) The lance itself often caused the rider difficulty, with the spear (head) or butt striking comrades in the confusion of battle. If the lance penetrated too deeply into its target then within seconds the lancer would be dragged from his horse as his opponent fell, since the weapon was attached by a leather wrist strap. This befell a Polish lancer at Albuera: "Ensign Hay was run through the lungs by a lance, which came out through his back, he fell but got up again. The lancer delivered another thrust, the lance striking Hay's breast bone; down he went and the Pole rolled over in the mud beside him."

(**Above & above right**) *Firearms drill from the saddle; these weapons were probably more useful for firing signal shots when on outpost duty than in the thick of battle.*

Although a lancer did have a reach advantage to enable him to get in the first blow of a charge, once he was in a mêlée surrounded by sabre-armed cavalrymen there was no room to wield his weapon. His only chance was to open up the distance between himself and his antagonists, wildly parrying sword cuts with the lance shaft until he could break free of the throng, or until his rear rank charged in with their sabres to support him.

Meeting the Vistula Lancers for the first time in 1811, William Tomkinson of the 16th Light Dragoons described how "The lancers looked well and formidable before they were broken and closed to by our men, and then their lances were an encumbrance." This bears out Fortuné de Brack's assertion that "lancers crowded by swordsmen are lost."

Another unpleasant aspect of the lance was that it put wounded men lying on the ground within easy reach.

At Albuera two officers of the 66th Foot were recorded in the regimental records as having been wounded by lance thrusts while already lying disabled on the ground. At Waterloo a lancer rode up to the fallen commander of the 12th Light Dragoons, Lieutenant-Colonel Frederick Ponsonby: "The fellow came up and said, 'You are not yet dead, villain?'" and ran his lance into Ponsonby's body. Surprisingly, he lived through this ordeal. General Sir William Ponsonby, commander of the Union Brigade of heavy cavalry, was not so lucky. During the withdrawal after their famous charge his horse became bogged down in the thick mud and he was captured. Upon some of his men attempting to rescue him, a lancer ran him through.

(**Right**) *Cavalry cloaks of the Napoleonic period were made very large and loose, so as to cover not only the rider but also his saddle equiment and part of the horse's back. This French pattern of 1813 was actually a capacious overcoat with sleeves and caped shoulders.*

(**Left & below**) *Two members of the Élite Company of the French 7th Hussars on patrol, working as always in a pair; they are riding through the forest of Fontainebleàu to the south of Paris.*

The regiments of hussars – of which there were between ten and 14 at various dates - were distinguished one from another by a complex scheme of differently coloured, faced and braided uniform items. The 7th, who served with the 5th in Lasalle's famous Infernal Brigade and performed prodigies in the long pursuit of the beaten Prussians after Jena in 1806, wore this combination of green, red, and yellow or gold. Since 1801 each light cavalry regiment had included an Élite Company – the first of the two companies of the 1st Squadron – which was the equivalent of the Grenadier Company of an infantry battalion, and wore a fur busby instead of the shako of the other companies.

The hussars were the peacocks of the army and, as already shown, their style was similar throughout all Napoleonic armies. It was a formalised development of what had originally been the folk costume of the Hungarian irregular cavalry recruited to resist the Ottoman Turks on the far eastern borders of Christendom. What had once been a simple animal-fur cap had become a tall, cylindrical bearskin busby or colpack with a colourful hanging bag top; a jacket and a fur overjacket fastened by buttons and cord loops had become the lavishly braided dolman and pelisse; the spare reins and lariats carried wound around the waist had become the colourful barrel-sash. In full dress they wore tight breeches with braided thighs; in the field these were covered with leather-reinforced riding overalls which fastened up the outside seam so that they could be put on and taken off without removing the boots.

(**Opposite**) *Sergeant-major – maréchal des logis chef – wearing his dolman open to reveal his red waistcoat; his rank is marked by the two chevrons above his cuffs. It is a common misconception that period cavalry all wore cuffed gauntlets: on campaign some regiments wore short riding gloves, the gauntlets usually being kept for full dress parades.*

(Right) *Three orders of dress for the 7th Hussars; from left to right:*

Stable dress, worn not only for working with horses but also for drill sessions. When actually mucking out the stalls a work smock of the same linen as the trousers would be more usual, with wooden clogs instead of boots.

Campaign dress, with the charivari (riding overalls) worn over the Hungarian breeches, and the fur-trimmed pelisse worn as a cold weather jacket. In warm weather the dolman would be worn alone, as on page 52, the pelisse being left with the unit baggage or at the depot. In 1806 an NCO's pelisse cost 112.50 francs, a private soldier's only 59 francs.

Full dress, with a plume mounted in the colpack instead of the pompon worn on campaign, the pelisse slung from the left shoulder over the dolman, close-fitting red Hungarian breeches, and the embroidered sabretache without its plain black campaign cover.

(Left) *The* Chasseurs à Cheval *of the Imperial Guard, the premier light cavalry regiment of the French army who provided Napoleon's mounted personal escort at all times, were uniformed in hussar style in green and red, with braiding in gold for officers and "dawn", a peach orange shade, for other ranks. (There was no Guard Hussar regiment.) Here a trumpeter and an officer prepare to mount up, the former wearing a high-visibility contrasting uniform of pale blue braided with crimson and gold and a white colpack. Chasseurs on duty with the Emperor were ordered to wear the scarlet regimental pelisse with the full dress breeches of yellow/buff deerskin so as to be easily distinguishable from other regiments.*

(Right) Chasseurs à Cheval *officer in bearskin colpack, dolman, barrel-sash and overalls. His dark green uniform is picked out with lavish gold bullion braid and cord and gilded buttons. Cavalry officers' pouch belts were of fine Morocco leather with heavy bullion embroidery and gilded fittings; it was common to protect them when on campaign by buttoning this kind of cover around them.*

(Below) Chasseurs à Cheval de la Garde *parade in the courtyard of the Musée de l'Emperi at Salon de Provence. The whole regiment wore the fur colpack, the distinction of the élite company in Line hussar regiments. Known as "Napoleon's favoured children" or "The Invincibles", the*

Chasseurs traced their origins to an élite bodyguard of Guides which the young General Bonaparte raised in 1796 during his Italian campaign. As he progressed to First Consul in 1799, and finally to Emperor in 1804, so their strength and title changed; but the surviving veterans of Italy and Egypt were still the nucleus of what became from 1802 a four-squadron regiment about a thousand strong.

The Chasseurs' duties were not confined merely to escorting the Emperor; they were also committed to battle, making particularly impressive charges at Marengo, Austerlitz, Eylau and Waterloo, and losing two regimental commanders and many other officers and men in action.

(Opposite) Lieutenant of Mounted Chasseurs of the Guard as he might have appeared under the early Empire. At that date a long-tailed habit coat with a cutaway front was the campaign dress for all ranks, and was retained for undress uniform for many years afterwards. All French junior officers wore a single epaulette; the aiguillette on the other shoulder was a distinction of the Guard cavalry regiments. The bicorn hat is correctly cut – the idea was to give impressive added height. Its ornaments were all originally practical, but had become formalised by this period: the laces which pulled the hat brim up and their tightening pulls are now gold tasselled strings, and the buttoned cord loop holding the national cockade in place is a large strip of gold bullion lace.

(Above) Many hussar units wore black shakos, but some were coloured. That worn by this officer of a centre company of the 5th Hussars is covered in light blue velvet to match the regimental jacket and overalls, furnished with gold lace, cord and tasselled raquettes; the line of gold rings round the top also marks officer status. The regiment's white pelisse is trimmed with thick fur and, like the dolman, is decorated with gold cords and three rows of gilt ball buttons; worn over the left shoulder (to keep the sword arm free), it fastens round the neck with a looped cord and toggle.

(Above right) A soldier of the same company; common cavalrymen had similar appointments and uniforms to their officers but invariably of poorer quality – this cording is of yellow worsted rather than metallic gold thread, and the shako cover is of woollen cloth. The brass scales facing the chinstrap and the brass edge to the visor gave some protection against sword cuts. In 1813-14 the 5th Hussars became even more colourful; they were one of several regiments which adopted a tall, cylindrical shako (the rouleau type) covered with scarlet cloth.

(Right) Sergeant of the 5th Hussars wearing bonnet, dolman and overalls. The single gold chevron above his cuffs marks his rank, and that on the upper left sleeve at least eight years service. The substantial tabs of cloth at the rear waist were supposed to prevent the swordbelt slipping down.

(Left) In dark green faced with rose, a lieutenant of the 7th Chasseurs à Cheval – the most numerous branch of the Line cavalry, with up to 28 regiments – chats to a captain of the 1st Polish Light Horse (later, Lancers) of the Imperial Guard. Both officers have tall parade plumes fitted to their headgear, and bullion-laced belts supporting a small pouch – originally for pistol ammunition, but by now largely ornamental. Note also the tight-cut trousers worn instead of breeches; these became popular with cavalry officers under the Empire. The subaltern of Chasseurs displays the buglehorn badge of that branch on his silver shako plate, and the simple kinski jacket worn from 1808. The Pole wears the blue and crimson lancer uniform with a plastron-fronted kurtka jacket and square-topped czapka cap.

(Right) Soldier of the Polish Lancers of the Guard, a volunteer regiment which earned a high reputation in battle. His uniform braid is silver, the other embellishments being of white worsted. Like the Vistula Legion lancers this unit retained the traditional Polish czapka, with a Polish cockade but also a sunburst plate bearing the crowned N for Napoleon. The stitching in the sides of the crown marks individual pockets each holding a small bundle of wooden slivers, and the top had an internal square of cane, diagonally reinforced; thanks to these strengthening features the cap gave a good deal of protection against cuts.

(Right) Red Lancer of the Guard. When the Kingdom of Holland was incorporated into the French Empire in summer 1810 the Dutch 1st Regiment of Hussars and the Horse Guards were amalgamated, and passed into Napoleon's Guard as the 2nd Regiment of Light Horse Lancers of the Guard (inevitably nicknamed les lanciers rouges *from their uniform*). By September 1811 their strength had risen to 1,406 men with 171 *Vélites* – volunteer officer candidates who paid to serve in the ranks while waiting to be accepted for a commission. Casualties of about 75 per cent in the 1812 Russian campaign (from which only some 60 officers and men returned still on horseback) destroyed the Dutch character of the regiment thereafter, and it was rebuilt largely with French cavalrymen, although a number of Dutch officers remained.

(Left) The Dutch cavalrymen in the initial formation of the regiment were renowned for their size, and it was even proposed that they became cuirassiers. However, given that the horses they ended up with averaged 14.2 hands it was perhaps as well that they were not employed as heavy cavalry, the weight of the big Dutchmen being enough in itself without the added poundage of a cuirassier's armour and equipment. It was apparently the regimental commander, General Edouard Colbert, who wished the lancers to be dressed in the Polish style, but in scarlet faced with blue and trimmed with yellow: nobody was going to mistake Colbert's regiment ...

A Saxon hussar picks dirt and stones from his horse's hoof at the end of the day's march.

The Napoleonic soldier of the Continental European armies was fighting, as often as not, against his country's true interests as part of an ever-shifting pattern of often forced alliances. He might even – like the Saxons in 1813 – be contributing to the rape of his own homeland. King Friedrich August of Saxony was forced to provide Napoleon with troops after being defeated in the 1806 Jena campaign. The hussars were raised during a reorganisation of the army along French lines in 1810; and were one of the units which formed VII Corps of the Grande Armée in Russia, where they suffered terrible losses. The avenging Russians rolled west into Germany; Prussia and Austria joined them; but it was not until the battle of Leipzig in October 1813 that the unhappy Friedrich August was able to separate himself from his terrifying ally and rejoin the coalition against France, by which time Saxony was utterly ruined.

A corporal farrier of French light horse replaces a shoe. These began life as long, straight metal bars, which were cut and hammered into shape using portable forges carried with the regimental supply wagons. Normal wear and hoof growth dictates that horses should be re-shod approximately once a month, but on campaign this was not always practical due to the pressure of time and the unreliable supply of the hundreds of thousands of horseshoes and millions of nails required by a large army during several months operations: for the want of a nail the war was lost ... Prolonged riding over rough ground might also cause a shoe to be cast – to work free – at any time; and Napoleon expected his cavalry to cover great distances with little rest.

The worn-out shoe was first removed with pincers, taking care not to damage the outer crust of the hoof. Excess growth was then filed down with a rasp. To judge if the filed surface of the hoof was flat enough to accept the new shoe the iron was first heated in the forge just hot enough to leave scorch marks on any raised areas, and then offered up to the hoof. These were then rasped down, and any necessary alterations made to the shoe on the farrier's anvil. A final check was made with the re-heated shoe, which could then be nailed into place. Nails were driven through the insensitive outer crust of the hoof and then bent over with the hammer to form the "clench". Carelessly placed nails could lame a horse, and not all army farriers were highly skilled and humane.

(Left) *Soldier of the Élite Company, French 7th Hussars, dismounting to lead his horse uphill. Horses were supposed to be led on steep slopes to prevent wearing them out, and should anyway have been led for a while at regular intervals. In practice care of the horses depended very much upon the individual regiment and especially upon the officers and NCOs enforcing the regulations. If a regiment was ordered to make a forced march to capture some vital bridge or stores depot before the enemy could destroy it; or if the cavalry were providing the rearguard during a desperate retreat, perhaps harried by clouds of Cossacks – then horses might well be ridden to death. Even during the 1812 summer advance into Russia Marshal Murat's 22,000-strong cavalry corps lost more than a third of their mounts to thirst, exhaustion and disease in the first month of the campaign, before any major battle had been fought.*

(Below) By 1803 Napoleon had carried out his plan to re-armour his heavy cavalry and 12 regiments of his 'gilets de fer' (iron vests) stood ready for action. There were also two carabinier regiments who did not receive the cuirass and helmet until 1809. The cuirass was obviously proof against sabre or lance, and could deflect musket balls which struck it from an oblique angle or at long range. Close up, however, the story could be very different. After the battle of Quatre-Bras on 16 June 1815 Lieutenant-Colonel Ponsonby of the 12th Light Dragoons examined one dead cuirassiers' armour and found it to be perforated by three balls, several other sets also having one or more holes through them: "I wanted to find out if these cuirasses were ball proof or not; this plainly shows they are not." There are a number of cuirasses in museums which show the effects of being struck by artillery canister or even small round-shot; these apple-sized holes conjure up grisly pictures in the mind's eye.

(Opposite & above) Cuirassiers and chasseurs exercising their horses on the beach at Boulogne. As well as constant attention horses also require exercise, even in peacetime and in the depots or camps, such as the huge encampment of the Grande Armée assembled at Boulogne for the planned invasion of England in 1805. When allowed to gallop horses will naturally race one another, and it is this genetic trait that has always caused cavalry charges to career out of control unless held in check by long training and tight discipline.

The cuirassiers were to provide the mass of decision, charging against demoralised enemy troops already weakened by artillery and infantry fire. The horses for the cuirassiers and carabiniers were supposed to be between 15¼ and 15¾ hands high, and the men were to be between 5ft 8ins and 5ft 10ins – at the upper end of the range of French manpower. Their weight could provide an essential impetus in the charge, and their fame went into battle before them:

"In drawing swords, my men threw back the right side of the cloak over the shoulder uncovering their cuirasses, and cuirassiers had a colossal reputation. So I observed a very distinct movement of hesitation in the head of the (enemy) column; some hussars moved to the rear, and this put their troops in disorder, besides they were coming up without keeping their ranks. The two dragoons with the officer whom I have mentioned before fired at me and missed me; I wounded one of them and passed on. We came to the hussars and literally passed over them. I do not think that four of them were left on their horses, they were so overthrown by us and by each other."

(Opposite) On the clifftop outside Boulogne a corporal (brigadier) of the 5th Cuirassiers, his rank marked by the two white diagonals above his cuff, exchanges the gossip of the camp with a farrier of the 2nd Dragoons – note the horseshoe sleeve badge. The cuirassier regiments all wore the same full dress uniform of blue jacket and chamois-coloured deer or sheep leather breeches with high boots, being identified by the colour and details of the facings. Their iron helmet had a brass crest and was embellished with a black hide or fur turban, a horsehair tuft and mane, and for parades a tall feather plume. The white-trimmed red lining prevented the edges of the armour chafing the jacket.

The dragoon wears the long-tailed green coat of that whole branch, again differenced by facing colours. Dragoon helmets were of the same pseudo-Classical shape, but of brass with a brown cowhide turban. As well as his straight sabre the dragoon carried a musket, thus this farrier's crossbelt equipment with a cartridge pouch and (obscured here) a bayonet. Note the bonnet de police carried in the usual infantry manner, rolled and strapped under his cartridge pouch.

During the Peninsular War the terrain exacted a heavy toll on the cavalry's horses. "We never off saddle except in the evenings, merely to clean the horses, and the men sleep in their appointments holding the reins," wrote Captain Tom Kinson in 1810. It takes a great deal of time to tack up a horse from scratch, and a regiment caught unsaddled, without equipment on horses and men, was lost.

Spanish roads, where they existed at all, were very stony, making for hard going on the horses' feet and legs; this, and lack of suitable fodder, all combined to reduce the horses' condition and thus the cavalry's effectiveness. Luckily for the British, over the other side of the hill the French were experiencing the same problems, in many cases to an even greater degree. The Royal Navy's dominance of the sea lanes saved the British cavalry from becoming as debilitated as the French by supplying remounts from Britain; but even so many horses perished on the voyage to the Peninsula.

Although orders had been published on horse care and feeding as early as 1795, little was to improve until these orders were enforced. Not all British officers took a serious interest in the boring details of mounted warfare, many leaving the chore of supervising stable duty to their NCOs, whose conscientiousness also varied. Depot squadron horses on home service were supposed to receive 14lbs of hay, 10lbs of oats and 4lbs of straw per day; when on campaign local foraging was supposed to supplement this ration, but neither army rations nor foraging were reliable and the horses suffered accordingly. Horses also suffered greatly from overloading;

the recommended load of one quarter of the horse's body weight or 250lbs was more often than not exceeded, causing the long-suffering beasts sore backs. The most intensive campaigning naturally took place in the summer months, and the harsh Spanish sun and sometimes parched terrain put water at a premium.

Some unscrupulous troopers even went so far as to sell their horses' rations to enable them to supplement their regimental alcohol allowance. Luckily this behaviour was punished severely whenever it was discovered, usually to the tune of one flogging for selling the fodder and another for being drunk. Drunkenness was behind most of the punishments inflicted on the private soldier.

The following extracts on stable duties are taken from the first standing orders of the 15th Light Dragoons, and give an insight into contemporary procedures when on home service:

"A stableman to be appointed for every six hours, their names to be wrote on the Stable Door & always to be in the way if wanted, his Principal Business to sweep out the Stable at the Proper Hours, put down the Litter at Eleven O'clock give Fresh Hay comb mains & tails &c. ...

"Every dragoon the Instant he comes into the Stable to hang up his Watering Cap & Cloaths & to put on whatever he has to keep him Clean whilst Dressing his Horse. Every man to rub his Horse's Legs before feeding with a Wisp of Straw in each Hand, he must therefore kneel on both knees. This for 10 Minutes at least at a Time ...

"All horses in the same Stable to be fed at the same time & this never to be done but in the Presence of an Officer,

or non Commis'd Officer. In a Stable without stalls each man to stand by his Horse while Feeding. The Hay is always to be well shaked before given to the horses. The More hand Dressing about the Legs, the Better, Care to be taken that the Horses have not too much Water in Cold Frosty weather, 2 Quarts in a Morning can be watered in the Course of their Exercise. No man is ever to leave his Stable till Dismissed by a Non Commiss'd Officer after the Inspection of the Officer and Qr. Master. When any Horse coughs & is Observed not to feed well the Non Commiss'd Officer will Immediately Report him to the Qr. Mar & Officers of his Troop. The same attention if the Saddle hurts him. The Litter to be in General Up in warm Weather and only Down after Exercise & at night. In cold Weather the Litter may be up till Eleven O'clock & then put down, the Horses Cloathes to be kept as Clean as Possible & therefore Washed & Scowered when necessary ...

"Hay that is Dusty or Mouldy should be sprinkled with Water and well shaked up with a Forks before it is given to the Horse. Great attention is to be given that no waste is made of the Forage. The Stables kept cold & free from any bad Smell as nothing more Contributes to the Health of a Horse when there are not proper air Holes, they must be made if possible. The Horses are always to be out in some shape or other when the Weather & other Circumstances don't prevent it. The less a Horse stands upon his Litter the better in general for his Feet ...

"The Qr. Masters to be very exact in the Attendance at all Stable Hours & in the General care of the Horses & to

the strict observance of the Orders of the Regiment. They will everyday Inspect the Shoeing and give the necessary directions for its being completed. When the Horses turn out in Watering order, they will always be present & if they go out of the Quarter, one Qr. Master at least, to be mounted, & to attend to the order, & riding of the Men ...

"The Horses tails to be Cutt, The first of every Month. The Legs are on no account ever to be touched with Scissors, Hand dressing will always clear away the Superfluous hairs, the Edges of the Ears, may occasionally be Clipt, but never inside, the long hair under the Jaws may be Singed (with a singeing lamp). The Qr. Masters to take account of the quality of Stabling, & No. of Inns, in every town, upon a March or wherever the Troop happen's to Quarter. The Adj't will take care to Collect them at proper times & enter them in the Regimental Book ...

"Half the Trumpets of the Quarters, to blow the Common Dutys, of Parades and Stables & going out in watering order. When the Troops turn out Mounted for Exercise, or a March, all the Trumpets are to blow from the Parade, or Commanding Officers Quarters & are therefore to be mounted & ready, ten Minutes before the time. The watch to be set by all the Trumpets of the Quarter. The Trumpets to be Instructed, by their Troops in the care of their Horses & putting on their Baggage. This they are always to do on a March & thoroughly to rub them down in coming into Quarters. Upon all Occasions they are to be obliged to keep themselves remarkably neat, clean & to be provided accordingly with additional necessaries for that purpose."

(Opposite and this page) Sergeant and soldiers of the British 12th Light Dragoons on the picket line in camp, wearing watering order (the NCO's sideburns are of the type French soldiers called "pistol butts"). Horses require constant care and attention, and grooming, mucking out, feeding and watering their mounts took up more of a trooper's time than did exercising and training. Hooves needed repeated picking out, eyes had to be cleaned, coats and tails brushed – the tasks were endless, for if a cavalryman was doing his job properly then the horse always came first.

Sore backs caused by the horse carrying too heavy a load of man and equipment were compounded by not off-saddling the horse often enough, causing poor circulation. Saddle sores were frequently the result, and the more so when not enough padding was placed between the wooden saddle trees and the horse's back. These sores not only caused the horses great pain and eventually made them unridable, but could also cause the horse to rear and throw the rider when pressure was applied against them. One officer recorded: "If once a horse gets the skin off his back on the march, it is all over with him; I have seen holes on horses backs that you might put your fist in within three days from the time that the skin was first rubbed off; notwithstanding this they were obliged to carry the baggage, for officers had no money to purchase others."

(Above) Horse tack consisted of saddle, bridle and assorted attachments. British light cavalry of the period used the Light Cavalry Universal Saddle whose basic structure is exposed here (provided they could obtain it, as equipment was only issued when older items were no longer serviceable). Designed in 1805, this was based upon the Hungarian-style "high mounting" saddle which was the fashion throughout Europe. This saddle was suspended above the horse's spine on two beechwood side boards and had strong front and rear arches; this design kept weight off the spine and distributed it across the back. To the flanks were detachable leather flaps; the rawhide seat (known as a "woof" or "wolf") was covered by a quilted leather "pilch" or cushion which was attached to the pommel (front) and the cantle (rear) by leather loops. Both pommel and cantle were reinforced with iron bands, but even so they were prone to breakages on active service, the metal being unable to stop the wood from splitting and the subsequent movement often injuring the horse's back. The saddle girth ran under the horse's belly; a chest strap ran around the breast, connecting to both sides of the saddle and to the girth to prevent the saddle slipping backwards. A crupper strap passed under the tail

and attached to the saddle to prevent it moving forwards.

Before the horse was saddled a thickly folded blanket was placed on its back to cushion the side boards, raised at front and back to allow a flow of air to the spine. If the blanket was not thick enough or was not correctly positioned then saddle sores would result. On campaign a sheepskin covered the seat for a more comfortable ride (not only horses suffer from saddle sores), a cloth shabraque being substituted for full dress occasions. Two drawbacks of the sheepskin were that on hot days it proved exceedingly warm, and on wet days it soaked up water like a sponge.

To the pommel were attached two pistol holsters, and often the rider's rolled cloak; and to the cantle two horseshoe cases and a valise – a cylindrical cloth case in which the rider carried his own necessities. A carbine boot was positioned to the right of the saddle; originally it held the butt of the carbine but later its design was changed to hold the muzzle, as it was difficult to prevent the carbine from moving while riding. Several different patterns of boot and strapping were tried, but most still caused chafing of horse or rider. In the field corn sacks, forage nets, nosebags, canvas buckets and picket stakes and ropes were also carried.

(Right) Double rein bridles were used to control the horse's head. Recruits were taught to ride with the leg and spur, but still many horses' mouths were spoilt by excessive use of the twin reins with snaffle and curb bits. In 1812 British light cavalry adopted a Hungarian pattern bridle featuring crossed diagonal face straps with leather rosettes. This example decorated with cockleshells is typical of an officer's more elaborate equipment. *(This bridle was cut to fit a larger horse than the one wearing it here. Horse furniture should be cut to size, and could be adjusted within a certain leeway; but given the number of horses lost in action, it is hardly surprising that not all horse equipment ended up a perfect fit).*

(Far left) All armies issued simple cloth caps and jackets for wear as stable dress or watering order. This French Chasseur à Cheval of a Line regiment wears the universal bonnet de police *with the buglehorn badge of his branch of service.*

(Left) After 1812 the nightcap-type bonnet was ordered replaced throughout the French army by this pokalem style, with a fold-down neck and ear flap. Again, it was made in the appropriate uniform colour for the branch of service; this trooper of the 1st Chasseurs displays his regimental number.

(Left) The saddlery of a soldier of the Red Lancers of the French Imperial Guard, with sheepskin (typically lined with coloured cloth cut in "wolftooth" or "vandyke style") and valise. The full dress shabraques were often seen with the rear corners turned up to protect the expensive embroidery; on campaign the dust and mud flung up by a marching army would soon discolour such finery. Another option, often taken by hussar regiments, was to leave the shabraques in their regimental depots.

(Below) The magnificent full dress sabretache and shabraque of an officer of the Chasseurs à Cheval of the Imperial Guard.

(Opposite) Every item of this Saxon hussar's dress and horse furniture has a practical purpose, but is coloured and decorated to make a strikingly handsome effect. Imagine 500 of these riders moving across the battlefield in close formation…

(Opposite) The Grenadiers à Cheval *(nicknamed the Black Horses, the Big Brothers or simply the Gods) were the premier heavy cavalry regiment of Napoleon's Guard. (When the Empress's Dragoons were added to the Guard in 1806 they were styled medium cavalry, although they aspired to obtain horses approaching the weight of the Grenadiers' mounts.) On campaign the Grenadiers often wore the simple surtout jacket, without the white lapels of the habit worn here by a senior NCO – note the mixed red and gold of his epaulette and aiguillette.*

Coignet records that during the battle of Marengo, 14 June 1800, "The splendid Horse Grenadiers came up at a gallop, charged the enemy at once and cut their cavalry to pieces. Together with the Chasseurs à Cheval de la Garde, the regiment had gone into action at the orders: Escadrons – en avant – marchez! ... Au trot! Cloaks diagonally fastened across their shoulders, sabres in hand, they advanced at a steady trot on their tired horses. Then 'to the right by files!', and finally, Au gallop! ... Chargez! – crashing into the Austrian cavalry which had been positioned to cover its infantry's retreat."

Sergeant Lanceleur and Grenadiers Millet and Leroy cut down enemy standard bearers and each captured an enemy flag, the height of glory for a cavalryman. After their success that day the Grenadiers were said to have slept in their saddles, still mounted on their exhausted horses.

In 1805 they were in action at Austerlitz: "Then the Emperor let loose his Black Horses, that is his Horse Grenadiers, commanded by General Bessières. They passed us like a streak of lightning, and fell upon the enemy. For a quarter of an hour there was a desperate struggle, and that quarter of an hour seemed an age to us. We could see nothing through the smoke and dust. We feared we should see our comrades sabred ... and as we were advancing slowly behind them, if they had been defeated it would have been our turn." Luckily for Coignet, "Our Grenadiers came off the victors, and returned to their position behind the Emperor."

In the final moments of Waterloo a British officer described this regiment "moving at a walk, in close columns and in perfect order; as if disdaining to allow itself to be contaminated by the confusion that prevailed around it."

(Above & right) *The British heavy cavalry consisted of the 1st and 2nd Life Guards – an officer is pictured here in the uniform worn from 1812 – the Royal Horse Guards (Blues), 1st to 7th Dragoon Guards and 1st to 6th Dragoons, along with the 1st and 2nd Regiments of the King's German Legion Dragoons. At Waterloo Major-General Lord Edward Somerset's 1st or Household Brigade comprised the 1st Life Guards (228 strong), 2nd Life Guards (231), Royal Horse Guards (237) and 1st King's Dragoon Guards (530). Sir William Ponsonby's 2nd or Union Brigade had three regiments each with three squadrons of two troops: 1st (Royal) Dragoons with 394 men, 2nd North British Dragoons (Scots Greys) with 391, and 6th (Inniskilling) Dragoons with 396. One source claims that by the general advance on the evening of the battle the two brigades combined could muster a fighting strength of a single squadron – about 100 mounted men out of 2,400 that morning.*

(Left) *Soldier of the British 12th Light Dragoons drawing his sabre, an awkward manoeuvre in the saddle while keeping the eyes to the front. Until 1812 light cavalry wore a laced dolman with a leather "Tarleton" helmet. After 1812 (in some cases long after, as regiments on foreign service took longer to receive new uniforms) they were issued with this plastron-fronted* kinski *in dark blue, with regimentally coloured facings on collar, cuffs, plastron and rear seam piping (see list in Appendix). The whole uniform was copied from elements of those worn by admired foreign cavalry: the bell-topped shako and the epaulettes from the French, the jacket and striped girdle from the Poles.*

(Right) *A good view of the cleaver-like cutting edge of the 1796 light cavalry sabre; and of the cap lines, attached to the jacket so that the shako would not be lost if it was knocked off.*

Although Wellington singled out the 12th LD for praise, on outpost duty most British light cavalry had a long way to go to catch up with the highly professional King's German Legion. Each regiment developed its own procedure, learning by experience: "Regular signals should be established throughout the cavalry, so as to be understood by all. At Gallegos, in 1810, we had the following: When the enemy appeared, the vedette put his cap on his carbine. When he saw only cavalry, he turned his horse round in a circle to the left; when infantry, to the right. If the enemy advanced quickly, he cantered his horse in a circle, and if not noticed, fired his carbine. He held his post until the enemy came close to him, and, in retiring, kept firing."

CHAPTER 3
OFFICERS AND GENTLEMEN

You need not hide, Sir. If there is anything there for you it will find you out. (Sergeant to a young officer in his first battle, running back and forth as if trying to dodge the shot and shell.)

In war one requires leaders, and in all Napoleonic armies the officer corps had an essential role to play, though the character and culture of each army might differ. In all the European monarchies there was still an entrenched belief that officers should be drawn from the aristocracy, and that qualities of leadership were inborn rather than taught. Outside Revolutionary France birth always mattered, though the degree to which it governed an officer's career prospects varied.

In Prussia, for instance, the 18th century Kings Frederick William I and Frederick II the Great had created an army with a high reputation for efficiency. Frederick the Great demanded a lot of his officer corps, but despite his military realism he was reluctant to commission men from outside the aristocracy. Nevertheless, a very promising middle class officer might be enobled in order to allow his advancement, and the many foreign-born officers employed by Prussia did not suffer this sort of discrimination. Scharnhorst, the gifted reformer who rebuilt the beaten Prussian army during the Napoleonic Wars, was the son of a Hanoverian artillery sergeant; and Gneisenau, Prussia's most brilliant staff officer, was the son of a respectable but impoverished Saxon officer. Yorck, one of Prussia's best fighting generals and a leading theorist of light infantry tactics, had actually been court-martialled and thrown out of Frederick the Great's army, and only regained his commission after the king's death; yet in 20 years he rose to senior command. The highest ranks of the Prussian army were certainly open to talent.

The army of Austria-Hungary was hampered by the bureacracy and the very conservative culture of the empire from which it was recruited. The multinational ruling classes were riven by political quarrels and factional manoeuvring. While officers from the higher aristocracy were fairly rare, they could buy direct commissions and rapid promotion. Most officers were from the lesser nobility and gentry, and had often served as cadets in the ranks of regiments before being commissioned. However, appointments of officers below field rank (i.e. up to captain) were still in the gift of the aristocratic "proprietors" after whom the regiments were named, thus ensuring advancement by social connection rather than professional talent.

With a few notable exceptions, usually of foreign background, the officer corps of the out-dated Russian army was, in the unanimous opinion of their contemporaries, completely useless for any but the most basic purposes. Senior rank was open only to the great aristocratic families; the lesser country gentry who officered the Line regiments were not seriously required to have any knowledge of their profession and had no hope of preferment, many being barely literate. Their only virtues were physical courage and, since they stayed with their regiments for many years, the

A Scottish officer of the 42nd Foot, the Black Watch; the shoulder wings identify one of the two flank companies. Each of the ten companies in a battalion had an establishment of one captain commanding and two subalterns – lieutenants or ensigns. Like their men, the officers of the Highland regiments tended to be drawn from smaller and closer-knit communities than was usually the case in English regiments, and were often from a handful of leading clan families well known to their men before they joined the army. These close links throughout the ranks paid high dividends in unit morale and discipline: if an officer or man behaved badly he knew the story would reach his family and neighbours.

ability to inspire the loyalty of their brave and endlessly enduring serf-soldiers.

Even in the more professionally demanding armies, while not all members of the officer corps were automatically drawn from the aristocracy, advancement was much easier for those who had the right connections. Wealth and family could take a young officer a long way. It was to be hoped that somewhere along the line military ability would emerge, but this was not always the case, and the over-promoted officer was a recurring player in the dramas of the Napoleonic years. Colleagues could only quietly hope that the really dangerous idiot would get himself knocked on the head, in the euphemism of the day, before he did too much harm.

With 20th century hindsight it is tempting to assume that a majority of the officers produced by this system must

have been incompetents. Closer study gives the lie to this, at least in the British army following the reforms instituted by the Duke of York after the disastrous 1795 campaign, and presumably in other armies to a greater or lesser extent. Unfortunately, many of the older officers who would hold senior command during the wars were too high up the ladder by that date for reforms to have much effect on their careers.

Firstly, the young lords and the (far more numerous) sons of the country squirearchy who joined the British army were not, simply by reason of their birth, unintelligent or lacking in character. Really contemptible dilettantes were not unknown but were rare in the British army. Their class were brought up to place supreme importance on personal courage and honourable behaviour; they lived in a fairly small world where every man's conduct soon became known throughout his social class and home region, and personal reputation mattered enormously.

Again, while money and connections (political more often than aristocratic) might secure rank within a regiment, promotion to appointments of higher responsibility was harder to obtain. There was intense lobbying and influence-bartering, of course, but important commands were seldom open to crude nepotism; or even to simple seniority, absolutely unqualified by the judgement of superiors. Ambition and cynicism may be almost universal in human affairs; but there were some serious-minded and patriotic generals, politicians and senior civil servants, and such men

cannot have been eager to give brigade, divisional and corps commands to well-connected fools whose failure would reflect on those who appointed and commanded them. The recorded exceptions are notorious, but there was a system of checks and balances, however nebulous it may appear from a distance of 200 years.

Finally, we may think that at the regimental levels to which he was able simply to buy access the Napoleonic officer did not need to be a military genius to perform his duties adequately. Such administrative paperwork as was unavoidable was largely dealt with by perfectly competent clerks and secretaries; the fact that the army worked as well as it did proves this to be so. His company or battalion might suffer discomfort or inefficiency from the laziness or thoughtlessness of a bad commander; but regimental officers seldom had opportunities to make really crucial decisions on their own initiative. (And if they did make a foolish choice and got their men killed, then they sometimes died with them, thus solving the problem permanently.)

Generals such as Moore, Wellington, Abercromby and Hill were masters of their profession, able, energetic and humane; they demanded much of their subordinates, promoted the best of them on merit, and had ways of getting rid of those who proved unsatisfactory.

An officer's most important duty was to lead from the front, showing courage and coolness under fire, and the great majority fulfilled this duty to a degree we may find astonishing. As long as they were just and fair-dealing, with

(Left) A company officer of the 9th (Norfolk) Regiment leads his men into action; note the Britannia badge on their belt plates, mistaken by the Spanish for the Virgin – thus the 9th's nickname of "the Holy Boys." In the opinion of the young French General Foy, who had first-hand experience, the quality of the officers who led British units in the Peninsula was generally excellent. It may be epitomised by Lieutenant-Colonel Cameron. Although suffering from ill health since before the war, he defied the surgeons and insisted on leading his 9th Foot at Bussaco in 1810. Although injured when his horse was shot from under him, he led the bayonet charge of his regiment which drove the French from the Bussaco heights, sword in hand. At Salamanca in 1812 (when he should have been on sick leave) he replied to the order to advance with the words "Thank you, Sir, that is the best news that I have had today." He then called to his men, "Now boys, we'll at them." Cameron was a hard disciplinarian, but was held in high regard by both his officers and men. In a tough age there was a desperate need for strong leaders, and memoirs make clear that the men understood that a

weak character was more likely to get them killed than a strong one.

(Right) An officer working thoughtfully at his desk in a temporary billet. Under the Foot Guards undress jacket he wears a colourful waistcoat – a very mild example of the wide personal choice allowed over such details: "As to ourselves, we might be rigged out in all colours of the rainbow if we fancied it. The consequence was, that scarcely any two officers were dressed alike."

Many British officers came from the relatively modest country gentry, the professional classes and military families, and cost was always a factor in their appearance. The daily pay of a regimental officer of Line infantry was as follows: lieutenant-colonel, 15s.11d.; major, 14s.1d.; captain, 9s.5d.; lieutenant, 5s.8d.; ensign (2nd Lt), 4s.8d. The battalion adjutant, usually a lieutenant, received 8s.; the quartermaster, 5s.8d.; and the surgeon and his assistant, 9s.5d. and 7s.6d respectively. A subaltern officer thus earned only five to six times as much as a private, or three to four times as much as a sergeant – hardly a staggering difference, given that the officer had to buy his own horses and all his clothing and equipment.

"frank and gentlemanly manners, and the total absence of what may be termed teazing those under their command," and above all as long as they showed themselves brave leaders in battle, then their men seem to have been entirely content to follow them. In the words of Rifleman Costello of the 95th, "Our men divided the officers into two classes, the 'come on' and the 'go on'."

In the British army officers' commissions were, for the most part, purchased in sequence. Thus a man must first purchase a vacant lieutenancy (a "pair of colours") in one regiment; then, if he could afford it when a vacancy offered, a captaincy in that or another regiment; and so on, selling his last step in turn to the next applicant approved by his colonel. The most senior man in the next rank down in that regiment had first refusal, but many private deals were done, with frequent exchanges between regiments. A lieutenant-colonelcy in the cavalry cost £4,982.10s, a majority £3,882.10s, a captaincy £2,782.10s and a lieutenancy £997.10s; the equivalents in the infantry were less, but all were very large sums, and no officer without a private income could hope to pay them out of his salary alone. Unless he could get a free step up in his regiment due to the death of superiors in battle, then a poor officer of great courage and ability might languish in the subaltern ranks until he was middle-aged.

There were some promotions from the NCO ranks on merit, such as a heroic Sergeant Newman of the 43rd Foot who distinguished himself on the retreat to Corunna, and

Sergeant Masterson of the 2/87th who captured an Eagle at Barossa. Given an officer's living costs, and the width of the social gulf, such a reward was a mixed blessing. Since they could never afford to buy a promotion, they usually sold out as captains at most. Many who made the jump became paymasters or commissaries – jobs not thought suitable for gentlemen, where they could be useful without suffering the worst expense and embarassment of regimental life. Major Cocks spoke for many officers when he wrote in a letter to his uncle, "I like to see a young man, on first appearing in the army, with the air of a gentleman and not of a sergeant-major." His observations on a military education are equally enlightening:

"The different branches of the profession require a degree of difference in education. The service of the Light Cavalry, in which I have always been bred, is nowhere taught in England, and beyond a few practical rules can only be learnt on service by reflection and observation in the field. The service of the line requires more routine, but I think this routine is better gained after a man joins than before it. For the artillery and engineers, previous theoretical knowledge is certainly necessary."

In the French service many officers had been appointed from the ranks following the turmoil of the Revolution, and several soldiers of humble birth would become Marshals of France. Although large numbers of the aristocracy fled abroad, some becoming officers in emigré regiments fighting for the

continued on page 80

(Opposite) *A war-worn veteran, perhaps one of the many commissioned former rankers who followed Napoleon's star and whose loyalty and courage lifted them to a new station in life. He wears the reasonably austere uniform of a headquarters staff captain, but his horse furniture and fine mameluke sabre suggest service as an officer of light cavalry – junior officers could rotate between regimental and staff appointments.*

The French staff structure was divided into two basic departments: the General Staff (Etat-Major) and the Commissariat (Intendance). Under the former, the Corps of Adjutant-Commandants provided divisional and corps chiefs- and assistant chiefs-of-staff, assisted by adjoints like this officer, who might be serving a tour on the staff of one of the massed cavalry divisions of the Grande Armée.

(Above) *Dressed in their full finery, the hussar officers were the flashiest members of the army; this paladin wears the hussar full dress of the Chasseurs à Cheval de la Garde Impériale. Their uniforms were accordingly the most expensive, and a captain in a hussar regiment could expect to pay around 1,500 francs, depending upon how much gold bullion thread encrusted his person … . In comparison a hussar soldier's dolman and pelisse were considered very expensive at 216 francs. When officers of his Guard were obliged to replace their wardrobes, upon a change of regulation uniform or after losing their baggage in Russia, Napoleon made large cash grants to compensate them; letters from officers of the relatively more simply uniformed Red Lancers suggest that such expenses could involve loans which drove a whole family into debt.*

(Right) *This officer of the 5th Hussars, strolling outside his billet for a smoke on a chilly evening, displays no less than three layers of gold-embroidered uniform: the fur-trimmed white pelisse, over the sky blue doman, over the red gilet or waistcoat.*

Allies, when the worst excesses of the Terror had passed a good many of the pre-Revolutionary officer class decided to stay and take their chances under the new regime – even some aristocrats, such as the future Marshal Davout. The proportion of French Napoleonic officers from the provincial middle class was greater than that of either aristocrats or former common soldiers (who were usually held back by their illiteracy). Once he had made himself sole master of the army Napoleon promoted on talent alone, and made concessions for officers without wealth and deserving but illiterate soldiers.

It is often said that Napoleon's officers were younger than those of other European armies; but apart from the unprecedentedly fast promotion to general rank of some of the outstanding heroes of the early campaigns this does not seem to have been true. In 1805, for instance, the average age of French officers is said to have been 39 for both captains and colonels, 37 for lieutenants and 32 for sous-lieutenants. This argues strongly that many former NCOs from the Royal army were wearing epaulettes under Napoleon – a theory born out by study of individual records.

Coignet, who was promoted into the *Grenadiers à Pied* of the Guard, was told by his officer to lie about his illiteracy; when asked if he could write he replied that he could, and was promoted to corporal. He was then given several recruits who, while being slovenly soldiers, were considered bright enough to teach the corporal his letters while he in turn smartened up their drill. Eventually Coignet rose to the rank of captain, another product of the meritocracy inherent in Napoleon's army.

The commander-in-chief of any field army was ultimately responsible for victory or defeat; those chosen by their monarchs or ministries for senior command thus carried a heavy burden. The unfortunate Austrian General Mack, completely outclassed and beaten by Napoleon at Ulm on the Danube in 1805, was sentenced to death, but this was reduced to imprisonment in an Austrian fortress (and he was later pardoned). The early French Revolutionary regime sometimes sent failed generals to the guillotine (such as General Custine in 1793 after his defeat at Valenciennes); but although this policy cost France the services of several good officers who simply fled the country, it was relatively short-lived, and largely due to hysterical suspicion about the loyalty of former Royal officers.

In the most conservative armies, such as those of Spain and Russia, powerful aristocrats might keep their commands despite repeated, even abject failures; but in more rational armies a serious defeat in open battle at equal odds usually meant the end of an active military career. The other side of the coin was that a string of successes could bring immense wealth and privilege. Napoleon famously rewarded his successful generals and marshals with riches and titles. British governments, administering a public exchequer rather than enjoying the luxurious freedom of a dictator, were a good deal more parsimonious with money; but titles and orders were prized, and could be the foundation of a family's long-term wealth.

Arthur Wellesley, first Duke of Wellington, was a special case. As a boy he was the apparent dullard among a family of
continued on page 86

(Far left) A French light cavalry general, decorated with the cross of the Legion of Honour and dressed in gorgeous regimentals; the hat, worn en colonne *or fore-and-aft, demonstrates why soldiers called generals "the feathers."*

(Centre left) Rear view of the long-tailed habit *which, in various different branch of service colours and with appropriate decorations, was almost universally worn by French officers at least until c.1812. This is that illustrated from the front on page 56, bearing the buglehorns of the Guard* Chasseurs à Cheval. *Note the typical cavalry officer's pouch on its covered crossbelt.*

(Left) Cuirassier captain in full dress. His tall dress plume, with a whalebone core, could cost up to 100 francs, as opposed to 3 to 5 francs for a soldier's shorter version. The horse cloth carries the silver grenade insignia of the cuirassiers, and has silver lace trim with red edging. Over his saddle and pistol holsters is a leopardskin shabraque edged with red woollen cloth cut into a "wolf-tooth" design; soldiers called such fur saddle covers "bedside rugs". To prevent his girth strap from rubbing against the horse's belly and causing galls he has wrapped a sheepskin sleeve round it. His bridoon rein is in white leather to distinguish it easily from the curb rein.

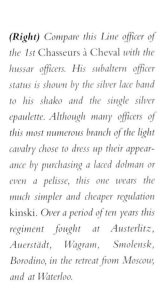

(Right) Compare this Line officer of the 1st Chasseurs à Cheval *with the hussar officers. His subaltern officer status is shown by the silver lace band to his shako and the single silver epaulette. Although many officers of this most numerous branch of the light cavalry chose to dress up their appearance by purchasing a laced dolman or even a pelisse, this one wears the much simpler and cheaper regulation kinski. Over a period of ten years this regiment fought at Austerlitz, Auerstädt, Wagram, Smolensk, Borodino, in the retreat from Moscow, and at Waterloo.*

A British major-general in the so-called embroidered uniform: several official orders of dress were allowed to general officers, and they augmented these with "any item that takes their fancy." This divisional commander is well mounted; boys of the class from which most British officers were drawn were brought up in the hunting field, and were thus experienced and often courageous cross-country riders before they joined the army. Generals of this period often led their men from the front, sword in hand; many died in battle, prominent among these being Ralph Abercromby, Robert Craufurd, John Moore and Thomas Picton.

Wellington was not always well served by his generals, however: "Really, when I reflect upon the character and attainments of some of my General Officers of this army, I tremble ... They are really heroes when I am on the spot to direct them, but when I am obliged to quit them they are children." Many were foisted upon him by the government due to political influence – men such as Sir William Erskine, whom the Duke understood to be a madman. Erskine was defended by Wellington's military secretary, Colonel Torrens: "No doubt he is sometimes a little mad, but in his lucid intervals he is an uncommonly clever fellow; and I trust he will have no fit during the campaign, though he looked a little wild as he embarked."

Out of 85 British general officers, only three were peers of the realm, and 21 the sons of peers or baronets; the others were either from the country gentry or had legal, clerical or service family backgrounds.

French generals and marshals often took the opportunity to display themselves in uniforms fitting their new station in life, perhaps won by the sword after fairly humble beginnings. They were a martial élite, and they wanted it to be apparent to all who saw them; horse artillerymen, for instance, such as this General of the Imperial Guard, copied the uniform style of the hussars. While this military splendour was the accepted fashion of the day there were still limits beyond which dandies became objects of amusement to their own soldiers. The most notorious example was the cavalry leader Joachim Murat, whose love of outlandish uniforms earned him the nickname "King Franconi" after the most famous circus of the day. It might be thought that singling himself out in this way put a general at unnecessary risk from enemy snipers, but in fact deliberately shooting at enemy generals was not considered honorable; many a distinguished career was cut short on the battlefield, but in most cases – such as Lannes and Bessières – they simply got in the way of a bullet or cannonball which could have hit anyone.

impoverished but ambitious Anglo-Irish gentry; his own mother sighed that he was "fit for powder and nothing else" ... but also that "Arthur has put on his red coat for the first time today. Anyone can see he has not the cut of a soldier." Yet he was to advance by sheer talent and determination to a pinnacle of military fame unique since Marlborough, and was to be raised in reward through every step in the British peerage while being showered with wealth and honours by grateful foreign monarchs. Nevertheless, if his successful command of the British and Allied army in the Peninsula had been interrupted by one severe defeat he would have been recalled, as he well knew. Fame won in battle could be a fleeting thing.

It was thus all the more important for a commander-in-chief to have competent and trustworthy subordinate generals, and here too Napoleon enjoyed a freedom of choice denied to his opponents. The Emperor – the military genius of his age – naturally led his army in person for the most important campaigns, and enforced his own judgement in operational planning. Even so, in an age before any battle-field communications and control system less primitive than a horseman carrying a message, once a battle was under way he was dependant on the varying talents (and luck) of his generals and marshals whom he seldom encouraged to show much initiative.

The same was doubly true when war on two fronts forced him to entrust far-flung operations to subordinates, like the luckless marshals who commanded in Spain. It was

during such episodes that it sometimes became painfully clear that some had been over-promoted; and others proved downright disloyal – the obvious examples are Bernadotte, Murat and Marmont.

For Wellington, who usually had to accept the subordinate generals appointed – often unwisely – by his government, the problem was worse. He seldom trusted them far from his eye, and he was usually right. Only the reliable and universally loved "Daddy" Hill, and the uniquely motivated Thomas Graham, proved trustworthy to command independent operations. At divisional and brigade level he had, over the years, many good fighting generals who simply followed his orders. He also had a number of bad ones who did not, most of whom he eventually managed to send where they could do little harm, if they were too well-connected to dismiss and too stupid to learn from his terrifying rebukes.

Although the staff work of the period seems primitive to us, it was as important to the outcome of campaigns as tactical leadership in battle. All Napoleonic armies needed a clearly defined command and staff structure (with the possible exception of the Russians, notorious for their inefficient staff work, whose operations seem to have unrolled by sheer human momentum, irrespective of calculation or cost). Strategy was the concern of the commander-in-chief; translating his intentions into specific orders, to flow down via corps and divisional commanders and to take form on the ground in the movements and tactics of brigades, regiments and battalions was the responsibility of the chief-of-staff.

Young, fast horsemen, superbly mounted on a chain of remounts (they usually owned several of their own horses), provided communication throughout a Napoleonic army. Often they were "gilded youths" of high birth who had obtained their appointments as aides-de-camp to their generals by personal recommendation. An ADC enjoyed a relatively comfortable life on campaign, since he lived and messed in the field as one of the general's immediate entourage. More importantly, being constantly under his commander's eye and carrying out his direct personal orders the ADC had many opportunities to make a good impression, and could hope for rapid advancement. However, the cost of this privileged position was often a series of near-suicidal missions, as the aide was sent repeatedly into the very heart of a raging battle to deliver orders. It was one of the most dangerous of jobs in any army. Wellington notoriously lost almost his whole "military family" to enemy fire at Waterloo, and spent the night after the battle on a makeshift bed while one of his aides died in the Duke's bedroom.

An aide-de-camp recalls a typically dangerous mission:

"My horse behaved splendidly, but his last day had come. In the hottest of the action, Marshal Lannes sent one of his least experienced aides-de-camp to General Saint-Sulpice with orders to charge with his cuirassiers a brigade of the enemy cavalry." Saint-Sulpice's horsemen then went off in the wrong direction; to correct this mistake Lannes called for another aide, but while he was explaining his orders a cannonball struck General Cervoni at Lannes' side, throwing him "stone dead against the Marshal's shoulder." Lannes continued to give orders with perfect clarity, though covered with Cervoni's blood. The aide redirected the cuirassiers; but in the action that followed, "my horse having received in the scuffle the point of a bayonet in his heart went forward a few steps, and fell dead against a corner stone in such a way that one of my legs was caught under the poor animal's body, and my knee pressed against the stone so that I was quite unable to move."

So, too, was the vitally important question of logistics. Keeping an army provisioned in the field, often over long lines of supply across hostile and poorly mapped country, mostly along dirt roads, with only horse-drawn transport and pack mules, was a fiendishly difficult task. If the system broke down then the army went hungry, or ran out of ammunition and remounts; and if the enemy had solved the problem better, then the unsupplied army faced at best a humiliating and costly retreat, at worst actual destruction. It was Wellington's far-sighted preparation of the depots and defences of Torres Vedras, more than his classic defensive battle at Bussaco, which saved his army and condemned Masséna's in the winter of 1810. Most notoriously, of course, it was hunger, exposure and lack of remounts much more than deaths in battle which reduced the Grande Armée of 1812 from some 450,000 men in June to about 10,000 effectives in December.

The value of talented staff officers was clearly recognized and as highly rewarded as the success of field commanders. Napoleon was fortunate throughout most of his career in having the services as chief-of-staff of Marshal Berthier ("the Emperor's wife"), an administrative genius who transformed Napoleon's strategic vision into the assembly and distribution of every kind of supplies, and the movements of hundreds of thousands of men and beasts.

Just because Napoleon's armies were notorious for plundering, we should not forget that his logistic system was infinitely better than anything which had gone before. In autumn 1805 Berthier and his small staff – again, relying almost entirely on message-riders – successfully organised the march of an army of 200,000 men from northern France to Austerlitz via Ulm and Vienna in just five weeks, and got it there in condition to win one of the decisive battles of history.

In the Prussian army General Gneisenau showed the same mastery of his immensely complex task; without him the brave but unsophisticated Marshal Blücher would have had no army to inspire. Wellington was famously reluctant to delegate, and was himself formidably educated and opinionated on the functioning of most corners of his command. He wanted no single chief-of-staff, and ran his army efficiently through three separate senior staff officers - whose functions may be simplified as staff communications (his military secretary), provisioning and movement (the quartermaster-general), and the organisation and management of the troops (the adjutant-general). Only the last had a higher rank than colonel.

But for all the planning, procurement, distribution, marching and countermarching, at the end of the day it was the regimental and battalion commanders who were at the sharp end. Upon them and their junior officers and NCOs rested the fate of all the illustrious personages who passed them at a distance like gods of war; and if their men ran, then all was lost.

OF FLAGS AND EAGLES

No corps may possess an Eagle which has not been bestowed by my own hand. (The Emperor Napoleon)
Raise high the black flags, my children! (Marshal Blücher)

Since at least the 16th century European military units had revived the ancient Roman tradition of carrying distinctive standards and flags on to the field of battle. Their practical purpose was to act as clearly visible rallying points in the smoke and confusion; but they also came to be seen as having a semi-mystical significance, embodying the history and pride of the regiment in physical form.

To capture the enemy's standard was not only to defeat him, it was to shame him. When an attack faltered the standard-bearer might push forward with suicidal courage, challenging his comrades to follow their own colours into danger for the sake of their honour. When disaster threatened, surviving soldiers rallied to their battle-tattered standard and closed around it back to back, preparing to sell their lives dearly. In the 17th century many flags had been carried, often by each separate company of a regiment. By the age of Napoleon there were various systems in place depending on nationality; in most armies regiments or battalions received standards.

In the British army the basis was the battalion. Each carried two standards on campaign: the King's colour and the Regimental colour. The King's colour was the Great Union flag, the national symbol, with an identifying regimental number added, and sometimes a traditional "Royal or ancient badge." The Regimental colour had a field of the regiment's uniform facing colour with the Union flag in the upper hoist canton (the top corner nearest the staff), and a regimental number and/or badge in a central wreath of roses, thistles and shamrocks, sometimes with additional corner badges. The staffs or pikes were about 9ft long and the flags 6ft 6ins square, and carrying them upright (particularly in a wind) was no easy task for the young ensigns traditionally honoured with the privilege.

It was also a perilous one, since the enemy concentrated their fire and their charges on the colours. In battle the ensigns were given an escort of half-a-dozen pike-armed sergeants (almost the only occasion when the sergeant's pike, with its long reach against attacking cavalry, was still a practical weapon). In a close action several ensigns and sergeants might fall around the colours, others always stepping forward to take their places. At the bloody battle of Albuera in 1811 two epic defences of the colours were recorded. As the French cavalry swept through the ranks of the 3rd Foot (The Buffs) the 16-year-old Ensign Thomas was surrounded; refusing to surrender, he was cut down and his Regimental colour taken, though it was later retrieved by the Fusilier Brigade. The bearer of the King's colour also fell wounded, and Ensign Latham sprang forward to steady it. A blow from a French sabre ripped through his face, another almost cleaved off his left arm above the elbow. Latham fell on the colour, and when the fighting had died down the flag was found under his unconscious body,

soaked with his blood and hidden inside his jacket. Although hideously disfigured by the sword blow to his face, and without his left arm, Latham survived and continued to serve. (He received a specially struck medal, and the Prince Regent, upon hearing of his bravery, personally paid his medical bills.)

The 57th (Middlesex) were subjected to "a most dreadful fire of artillery" at Albuera; their King's colour was shot through 17 times and had its staff broken, and there were 22 gashes in the Regimental colour. While Colonel William Inglis was urging his men to "Die hard!" he was cut down by a canister shot which smashed through his left breast, lodging in his back. He refused all offers of help, and lying on the ground he continued to encourage his "Diehards" – as the Middlesex were ever afterwards known – to hold their ground.

★ ★ ★

At the start of his reign Napoleon decided against employing the Gallic cockerel as his emblem. He adopted instead the eagle, as more majestic and also reminiscent of the eagles of Imperial Rome. Throughout the Empire it was the Eagle standard atop the staff which was important, and not the tri-

colour flag below bearing the regiment's title and battle honours – often the flag was rolled round the staff and protected by a cover when in the field.

The Emperor had an instinctive grasp of the management of morale among his troops, and emphasised the quasi-religious quality of the Eagle touched by his own hand as part of his cult of personality; the inscription on each flag included the words "From the Emperor of the French to the ..th Regiment." The colour party were to be men of long and excellent fighting record; the junior officer who carried the Eagle was escorted by two veterans from the ranks, promoted to the senior NCO status which would otherwise be unattainable for them by reason of illiteracy. These 2nd and 3rd Eagle-Bearers were armed with halberds and pistols, and usually wore Grenadier distinctions.

Eagles, naturally enough, attracted legends; they may not all be true, but some are convincing, and all emphasise the standard's perceived importance.

At Austerlitz in December 1805 the Eagle of the *Chasseurs à Pied* of the Imperial Guard was almost taken by the Austrians. Legend has it that Moustache, a mongrel poodle which had been the pet of the Eagle-Bearer of the 1st Battalion, stood guard over his dead master's body. When three Austrian soldiers rushed forward to capture the fallen standard Moustache joined the two surviving members of the escort, growling savagely and lunging at one of the Austrians, who slashed at him with his hanger and cut off one of the dog's paws. Despite this Moustache kept the Austrian at bay until help arrived, and the Eagle was saved. When Marshal Lannes heard about this he ordered a silver collar for Moustache with a medal commemorating the dog's bravery. Moustache continued with the army until he was killed by an English cannonball at Badajoz, and was buried on the ramparts.

At Eylau in February 1807 the 9th Light Infantry were in the forefront of the fighting, and four bearers were killed in defence of their Eagle. Four times the standard was captured from the dead hands of its guards by the Russian infantry, and four times it was retaken. The fifth bearer fell in a furious hand-to-hand struggle, and the 9th Light were forced back in disorder. Their officers and NCOs soon rallied them, however, and once more they went forward into combat with the fury of despair.

Now it was the turn of the Russians to withdraw, and the 9th took the village of Psarre Felden. Here, while searching for cartridges in the enemy's ammunition wagons to replenish their empty pouches, an officer came upon the lost Eagle, which had been snapped off its staff in the last desperate fight. The flag was missing and was never recovered, but the 9th Light had regained their honour, hurriedly remounting their Eagle upon a hop pole. The lieutenant who found it had earlier led one of the charges which had previously recovered it; and for both deeds he was awarded the Cross of the Legion of Honour and a cash grant.

Typically, Napoleon mentioned the regaining of this eagle in his 55th Army Bulletin, but without mentioning the exact manner of its final recovery:

"The Eagle of the 9th Light Infantry was taken by the enemy, but realising the deep disgrace with which their brave regiment would be covered forever, and from which neither victory nor the glory acquired in a hundred combats could have removed the stigma, the soldiers, animated by an inconceivable ardour, precipitated themselves on the enemy, routed them, and recovered their Eagle."

In the same battle the Eagle of the 30th Line Infantry was saved by Fourrier Morin. Although severely wounded and surrounded by his fallen comrades, he managed to bury the Eagle under the snow, fainting from loss of blood soon afterwards. It was the next day before he was found, but he had just enough strength to point out to his comrades where the standard lay hidden before dying from his severe wounds.

It was also at Eylau that a shell landed in front of the Eagle party of the *Grenadiers à Pied de la Garde*. The explosion smashed the staff in two places, knocking it to the ground in front of the Russians. Lieutenant Morlay, the 1st Eagle-Bearer, leapt forward to recover it and jammed the remaining stump of staff into the muzzle of a Grenadier's musket, carrying it thus for the rest of the day.

Captain Ernest Auzoni hurled himself at the head of a small group of Grenadiers into the heart of a Russian battalion and, allegedly shouting "Courage, brave comrades! Follow me!", led his men in the capture of the enemy's standard. Napoleon witnessed this, and later summoned Auzoni and the men of his company before him: "Captain Auzoni, you well deserve the honour of commanding my veteran Old Moustaches; you have most nobly distinguished yourself. You have won an Officer's Cross and an annuity of 2,000 francs. You were made captain at the beginning of this campaign, and I hope you will return to Paris with still higher rank. A man who earns his honours on the field of battle stands very high in my estimation."

Auzoni did not live to enjoy his new honours, since he was killed later in the day attempting to capture another Russian standard. We may doubt the theatrically perfect dialogue of his account, but Vauliancourt is convincing enough when he describes the scene next day when Auzoni was found: "About 150 or 200 French Grenadiers were lying dead, surrounded by four times their number of Russians. They were lying weltering in a river of blood, amid broken

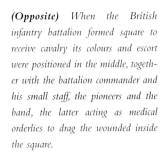

(Opposite) When the British infantry battalion formed square to receive cavalry its colours and escort were positioned in the middle, together with the battalion commander and his small staff, the pioneers and the band, the latter acting as medical orderlies to drag the wounded inside the square.

(Right) Officer and NCOs with the King's colour of the 42nd Foot, the Black Watch. Here they wear the full Highland uniform; on prolonged campaigns in the Peninsula Highland units often ran out of material for kilts, and made tartan cloth up into trousers (trews) instead. They also tended to run out of feathers for mounting their bonnets, and wore them without.

(Far left) Yellow cap bands and collars identify a Silesian unit of the Landwehr, the patriotic militia who rose to fight the French alongside the rebuilt Line units during Prussia's War of Liberation in 1813. Landwehr were not officially supposed to carry colours, but a number of home-made designs did exist.

(Left) Austrian Grenadier with the single colour carried by each of a Line regiment's battalions from 1808. The yellow field shows this to be the Ordinärfahne carried by battalions other then the 1st Bn, which carried a white Leibfahne.

(Opposite below) From 1809 Italy, now dominated by France, issued one flag per battalion with a basic design resembling the French 1804 pattern with their own national colours and motifs.

(Right) Before 1807 each Prussian Line infantry battalion carried two colours (four per regiment); the rebuilt army of 1813-15 carried only one per regiment – the premier colour of the 1st Bn, known variously as the Avancierfahne or Leibfahne. The colours varied in a small range, and certain details also differed, but the basic design for all units was as here. The blue oval cartouche beneath the national eagle motif carries the battle honour "Colberg 1807" awarded to certain regiments.

gun carriages, muskets, swords, and other debris. They had plainly fought with the most determined fury, for every corpse showed numerous and horrible wounds. A feeble cry of *Vive l'Empereur!* was heard as we rode up. It came from the middle of this mountain of dead, and all eyes were turned instantly to he spot whence the voice proceeded.

"Half concealed beneath a tattered flag lay a young officer whose breast was decorated with an order. He was still alive and though covered with many wounds, as we stopped by him he managed to raise himself so as to rest on his elbow, but his handsome face was overcast with the livid hue of death. He recognised the Emperor, and in a feeble, faltering voice exclaimed: 'God bless your Majesty! Farewell, Farewell! Oh, my poor mother!' Then he died. Napoleon seemed riveted to the spot." Auzoni's annuity went to his mother, although it is doubtful that she appreciated the exchange.

Napoleon was perturbed by the loss of his Eagles. As more were captured by enemy action he attempted to rationalise and minimise their loss by restricting the numbers issued to each regiment, decreeing on Christmas Day 1811:

"I only give now one Eagle per regiment of infantry, one per regiment of cavalry, one per regiment of artillery, one per regiment of special gendarmerie. None to the departmental companies or guards of honour. No corps may possess an Eagle which has not been bestowed by my own hand. Furthermore, all regiments of whatever denomination, if they did not receive the Eagle they are authorised to possess from the hand of the Emperor in person, either directly, or through a regimental deputation, must return it to the Ministry of War for the will of His Majesty to be declared ... . All other corps are to carry *fanions* (ordinary flags). Infantry regiments reduced below 1,000 men in strength and cavalry regiments of less than 500 men cannot retain their Eagle, and must return it to the depot. They will be accorded a flag *(drapeau)* without the Eagle. All the infantry regiments now in possession of an Eagle per battalion, and cavalry with one per squadron, are to send the extra-regulation Eagles at once to Paris, to be kept at the Invalides until they can be placed in the Temple of Glory (the church of the Madeleine)."

Knowing full well the weakness of his hastily rebuilt conscript units after the Russian disaster, Napoleon refused to give any Eagles at all to the regiments of 1813 until they had proved their worth on the battlefield: "No newly raised regiment is to receive an Eagle until His Majesty has been satisfied with its service before the enemy."

(Opposite) *Senior NCO of the 5th Cuirassiers carrying the 1804 pattern Eagle standard for cavalry squadrons, measuring 60cm square; those of dragoons and horse artillery were swallow-tailed guidons 60cm x 70cm. From 1812 only one standard was carried by each regiment, but the flags of all Eagles acquired a list of battle honours. Those embroidered on the reverse of the 5th Cuirassiers standard were Ulm, Austerlitz, Jéna, Eylau, Eckmühl, Essling and Wagram.*

*(**Above & right**) Reproduction of the gilded bronze Eagle and tricolour flag of the original 1804 pattern, in this case bearing the badge and inscription of the 1er Chasseurs à Pied of the Imperial Guard. Infantry flags were 80cm square. Despite the importance of the Eagle some soldiers irreverently called it "the cuckoo."*

In Napoleon's Imperial Guard no opportunity for a splendid martial display was ignored, such as this richly embroidered trumpet banner carried by a trumpeter of the Horse Grenadiers of the Guard, his contrasting sky blue uniform making him instantly recognisable in battle when his officer needed to pass an order by call.

Senior NCO of the Horse Grenadiers of the Guard carrying their superb 1812 pattern of standard, complete with crowns, Ns, Bonaparte bees, and battle honours. By the following year all Old Guard standards carried the honours "Marengo, Ulm, Austerlitz, Jéna, Eylau, Friedland, Eckmühl, Essling, Wagram, Smolensk, Moskowa, Vienne, Berlin, Madrid, Moscou." There cannot have been many regiments in history entitled to record entry into four major foreign capital cities – a fact which helps put Napoleon's extraordinary career in perspective.

During the pursuit after the battles of Jena and Auerstädt in 1806 the French 7th Hussars captured seven Prussian cavalry standards: those of the Anspach and Bayreuth Dragoons, the Queen of Prussia's Regiment, and four standards of the Light Cavalry of the Guard. Lannes presented his Emperor with 40 Prussian colours taken between Jena and Berlin; Soult and Bernadotte together sent 82 more. This was the scale of destruction that could be inflicted on a beaten and retreating army by vigorous and merciless pursuers. The like was never to be seen again.

CHAPTER 5

A HARD POUNDING

It is with artillery that one makes war. (The Emperor Napoleon)

When it was discharged I caught sight of the ball, which appeared to be in a direct line for me … I think that two seconds elapsed … until it struck the front face of the square. It did not strike the four men in rear of where I was standing, but the four poor fellows on their right. (Ensign Leeke, 52nd Foot)

Napoleonic artillery was often described as the Queen of the Battlefield. Napoleon, an artilleryman himself, was notable for employing heavy concentrations of guns to soften up a section of the enemy line prior to an assault by infantry or cavalry. Other commanders tended to place their batteries in more dispersed positions at intervals along their infantry lines. A well-sited artillery defence could shred an attack at close range with canister shot.

Gun batteries were categorised as either horse or foot artillery, although both were naturally dependant on teams of horses to draw the guns and their ammunition wagons. The distinction was between heavier, slower units whose crews marched, and fast, light units whose gunners rode horses or the gun limbers and who could therefore accompany cavalry.

Guns (long-barrelled weapons firing on a flat trajectory) were classified by the weight of the shot they fired; howitzers (shorter-barrelled weapons which could lob projectiles on a high trajectory) were classed by the diameter of their bore. Heavy "artillery of position" used 16-pounder, 18pdr and 24pdr guns and 8-inch and 10in howitzers, all of which were effective for bombarding fortresses. For use in the field the 12pdr was the heaviest easily transportable piece, as used by the foot artillery of Napoleon's Imperial Guard; these were often kept in reserve artillery parks until deployed to strike at decisive points. Field foot and horse artillery mostly used 6pdr or 9pdr guns and smaller howitzers. Artillery was grouped into batteries each of six to eight pieces, usually four or five guns and one or two howitzers, with their attached limbers and ammunition caissons.

Firing of guns was by direct line of sight; the recoil meant that the gun commander had to re-lay it by eye after each shot. Ideally, on firm ground, a solid cannonball would strike its first graze at between 300 and 600 yards, bouncing in front of its target and then continuing to skip forward through anything in its path, including flesh and bone – even a rolling ball had enough impetus to smash an unwary foot. Single roundshot hitting a closely formed body of infantry would kill and

(Opposite above) British 6pdr. gun, here surrounded by both foot gunners of the Royal Artillery in blue infantry-style uniforms with shakos, and cavalry-uniformed crewmen of the Royal Horse Artillery wearing braided dolman jackets, overalls and fur-crested Tarleton helmets. They hold double-ended sponge/rammer staffs; and the wooden lever used for aiming the gun can be seen sticking up from the trail. Manhandling guns took big men, and the strongest recruits were selected for this branch; a 6pdr weighed about three-quarters of a ton, a 9pdr a ton and a quarter, and a 12pdr nearly two tons.

(Left) Reconstruction of a Gribeauval cast bronze field gun; Napoleon's infantry called the artillery "the bronze", or "the brutal". Each gun had its own tools and water bucket hooked on, and an ammunition chest on the trail – its pitched lid can just be seen here – holding up to 15 rounds for immediate use. Each of the accompanying caisson wagons carried another 50 or 60 rounds, a spare wheel and a tool kit.

maim half-a-dozen or more (the record may be 26 men of the 40th Foot, reported by an officer at Waterloo).

Solid roundshot was used for long range bombardment of solid masses. When the enemy came closer you could change to heavy canister – three or four dozen large iron balls packed in a tin which disintegrated upon firing, belching a lethal cone of iron. For closer work light canister was used, a tin packed with 100 to 200 musket balls; fired at point blank range it could tear away the front ranks of approaching enemy units like a giant sawn-off shotgun.

Howitzers could also fire explosive shells detonated by a burning time fuze; and from 1804 British artillery alone had the very effective and disconcerting "spherical case", also known by the name of its inventor Henry Shrapnel. This was a thin iron casing filled with gunpowder and musket balls; if its time fuze was correctly cut it exploded above the intended target, showering them with lead. As a guide to the proportions carried, shrapnel was issued as 15 per cent of gun and up to 50 per cent of howitzer ammunition.

Another British invention was the Congreve explosive rocket, first used in 1805. The explosive and incendiary heads were effective for bombarding area targets, like a town (the heaviest was a 32pdr, with a range of up to 2,500 yards); but in the field it was anyone's guess where rockets would end up, as their flight path was usually erratic. The Russian General Wittgenstein called them "the devil's own artillery", and their effect on enemy morale could be spectacular, if only you could hit them in the first place. Wellington believed them to be useless to him as he did not wish to set fire to any towns, and regarded the RHA Rocket Troop sent out to him in January 1813 mainly as a valuable source of fresh horses.

The maximum range for all guns was about 1,000 yards (the powder charge was proportionate to the weight of the shot fired, and elevation angle and wind naturally affected the flight); and short range for roundshot was considered to be 450 yards. Heavy canister could be fired at 250-500 yards, light canister at under 250 yards. Maximum range for common shell was 1,700 yards, and for shrapnel 1,100 yards.

It was rare for a battery to open up at extreme range, as the relative inaccuracy of smoothbore cannon made this a waste of ammunition. Counter-battery fire was a temptation if ones own troops came under bombardment, but this too could quickly deplete ammunition stocks for little return; at Waterloo Wellington expressly forbade it. If properly deployed an enemy battery represented a widely dispersed target: a gap of 50 metres should have been maintained between the firing line of guns and limbers and the first row of caissons, and another 50 between the first and second line of caissons, which exchanged position as the ammunition ran out. The rest of the battery wagons lay another 60 metres to the rear. By contrast, undeployed batteries still hitched up to their teams and with their wagons in a traffic jam made valuable targets for enemy artillerymen.

The French had the excellent Gribeauval series of guns, howitzers and wagons, all designed with compatible fittings and common spare parts. An attempt to replace these by the "system of Year XI" (1803), was a failure. When the invasion of Russia began in 1812 many of the Grande Armée's cannon were of the new pattern (although forces in other theatres continued with the Gribeauval models). However, Marshal Marmont's artillery committee had rushed the Year XIs into production without enough testing, and the tried and true Gribeauval system was officially reintroduced in 1818.

The largest number of guns that Napoleon ever fielded was at Leipzig in October 1813: 600 pieces, or a ratio of three per thousand men in his army. Unfortunately, the assembled Allies were able to field 900 guns in reply.

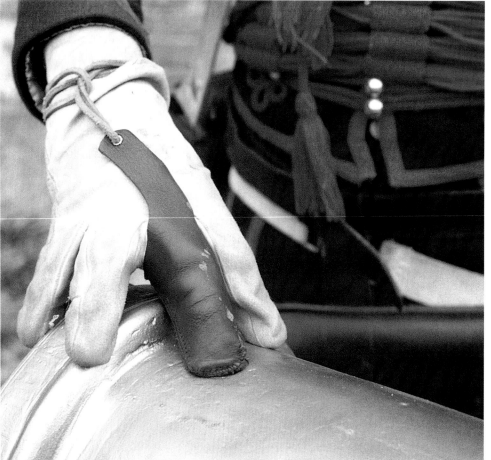

(*Above & left*) *French* Artillerie à Cheval, *in the smart light cavalry-style uniform adopted in 1812, training at gun drill. In battle the crew would number six or eight, with extra ammunition carriers from nearby infantry units. Here, after firing, the No.2 man swabs the barrel with a wetted sheepskin sponge to extinguish any powder sparks or smouldering fragments of cartridge; while he does this the No.4 or ventsman blocks the touch hole with his finger protected by a leather stall, to prevent a rush of air pressure fanning an ember into life. Failure to swab carefully could lead to premature explosions when the next powder charge was rammed home, with lethal consequences.*

The No.3 man stands to the right, carrying the next round for loading in his large leather satchel. He is kept supplied from the caisson by a relay of ammunition carriers.

(Right & below) The No.3 inserts a roundshot into the muzzle.

This is attached by tin straps and tacks to a wooden sabot, and this to a pre-weighed powder charge in a flannel bag; this will burn almost completely away at the moment of detonation. The No.2 man at the muzzle will now reverse his staff and use the wooden rammer end to push the round down to the breech end of the barrel.

The ventsman will then push a brass spike down the touch hole to pierce the powder bag; and will insert a fuze – a quill or a tube of some other light material packed with powder.

After laying the gun – aiming it by levering the trail round with a handspike, and elevating or depressing it with a screw under the breech – the sergeant signals to the gun commander, No.1, who ignites the fuze using smouldering matchcord on a staff (portfire); the detonation of the charge is almost instantaneous. Experienced gunners, with plentiful ammunition close to hand and no casualties among the crew to force them to double up on the different tasks, could keep up a rate of between one and two shots a minute. In reality no men or equipment would be immediately behind the gun, as the recoil from a full military load could be savage. The Nos.2 and 3, whose stations were at the muzzle, also had to move back behind it, and it was wise to cover the ears and open the mouth to protect the eardrums against the considerable air pressure. "One man of our company, in charging a field piece, was struck down by the wind of the ball, and which although it did not touch him, brought blood from his mouth, nose and ears; he never after thoroughly recovered from the effects of it."

THIS EVERLASTING CLOG

Marriage must be discouraged as much as possible (The Rules and Regulations for the Cavalry, 1795)

Her conduct was the theme of the army and she won universal praise and admiration. She was a perfect heroine. (Gronow, writing of the wife of Major Lord Waldegrave, 15th Light Dragoons)

Throughout history there have been few hardier souls than the women who followed the drum and marched alongside the vast hosts of the Napoleonic Wars. Soldiers' wives and sweethearts, gently bred officers' ladies, generals' flashy mistresses and common whores – all alike shared the hardship of the march, the discomfort of the bivouac, the dangers of the retreat, and the horror of the battlefield. Many carried their infant children across a continent at war; many gave birth by the roadside; and many perished wretchedly. Some officers (like Captain Wall, whose view of women on campaign is quoted as the title of this chapter) thought their straggling on the crowded route of march an unmitigated nuisance; other soldiers, of all ranks, spoke of them more gratefully.

Even in peacetime the lot of army wives was hard. In Britain there were virtually no barracks before 1792, most soldiers being billeted in small parties in inns and lodgings. A major building programme had produced about 200 barracks by 1805, accomodating some 163,000 troops, but not in any comfort, and certainly with no provision for married quarters. Up to 20 men shared a stuffy room, sleeping two or even four to a "crib" on a broad shelf running round the walls; those few soldiers who got permission to bring their wives on to the ration strength had no privacy but a blanket rigged up as a curtain. The same crowded room served for living, sleeping, cooking, eating, cleaning of kit, gambling, drinking, brawling and smoking – and such rudimentary washing as might be done by those discouraged by the cold pump out in the yard.

Sergeant Donaldson tells us how at night the room they slept in was "... cleared, and the forms ranged around. An old Highlander in the room had a pair of bagpipes, which, with two fifes, constituted our music, and when we were all assembled, the drinking commenced, handing it round from one to another. After a round or two, old Donald's pipes were called for, and the men commenced dancing with the women of the company. The stamping, hallooing, and the snapping of fingers which ensued, intermingled with the droning sound of the bagpipes was completely deafening.

"In the confusion some of the thirsty souls took the opportunity to help themselves out of their turn, which, being observed, caused a dispute; and the liquor being expended, a join of a shilling a man was proposed to carry on the glory. I was again applied to, and aided by this fresh supply they kept up the spree until one oclock in the morning. When some of them who had got drunk began to fight, the lights were knocked out, and pokers, tongs and tin dishes were flying about in every direction. At last the affair ended by the officer of the guard sending some of them to the guard house, and ordering the others to bed."

Redcoats of the 68th (Durham Light Infantry) fall upon a pieman's stall in the streets of a British port while awaiting embarkation. Their available pay per week was, after deductions, perhaps 1s.6d. (18 old pence), or by direct comparison 15p. Exact comparisons are deceptive, however, since the structure of prices for most goods has changed completely over 200 years. The purchasing power of a soldier's pay was perhaps 30 times greater for some goods, and much more than that for food and drink. However, it was never intended to be a wage on which a man might keep a wife and children.

Of the women in barracks Donaldson also wrote: "They were assailed with every temptation which could be thrown in their way, and every scheme laid by those who had rank and money, to rob them of that virtue which was all they had left ..."

When a battalion was ordered overseas six women per hundred were chosen by lot to accompany their husbands' units. As for their rations, officially "All men shall have one pound of biscuits and one pound of meat every day, with wine if the meat is salt. The women shall be on half rations and no wine however salt the meat." It was up to their husbands to provide anything else their families needed out of their pay. The women of a battalion could also provide for themselves by services such as sewing and laundering, for which they were paid a small amount; in 1794 *The Standing Orders for the Army in Ireland* gives the amount paid to a laundress in the Rifle Corps as 5d. per week for each individual soldier's bundle of washing.

continued on page 109

(**Left**) *The night watch goes about the street, checking the billets. When parties of soldiers were billeted on taverns and lodging houses the army undertook to pay the landlord to provide food, fuel and candles. Some soldiers made their landlords' lives a misery, bullying them into providing more than had been agreed; some landlords cheated illiterate soldiers out of the little they were entitled to.*

(**Below**) *A Polish Lancer of the Imperial Guard makes friends with two locals; a lady of negotiable affection was a* grisette *(roughly, "a tipsy"), or a "cartridge pouch."*

Much more respected were the French army's vivandières, *sutlers licensed to accompany a regiment on campaign, selling from their carts drink, tobacco, extra food, sewing and laundry services. They wore a license medallion around the neck, and a jaunty mixture of civilian and military clothes; captured hussar pelisses, brought to them by soldiers in exchange for a cup of brandy, were favourite garments. Often married to a regimental NCO, some became legendary for their loyalty and hardihood, like the great "Wooden-Head*

Mary" of the Guard Grenadiers, who was just one of hundreds who lost their lives. Mother Eugénie of the 10th Dragoons, wounded at Lützen in 1813, lost her twentieth cart at Waterloo. Perhaps the greatest was Catherine Rohmer, orphaned at the age of eleven when her sutler mother was killed at the battle of Fleurus. She married the drum major of the 62nd Line; served in Spain, at both Saragossa and Gerona, where she fought with a musket; was wounded at Wagram; survived Russia; was at Brienne and Montmirail in 1814, and accompanied her husband – now a member of the Sacred Battalion – to Elba, and back again to Waterloo. She bore 12 sons, and by the time she died had lost four of them and two husbands in battle.

(**Opposite**) *Walking out – two "Messieurs" of the Guard Grenadiers, very conscious of their superior status, stroll in search of a dockside tavern, and perhaps later the "Street of the Flying Lice" for some female companionship. (The ship is the restored frigate HMS* Trincomalee, *built in 1817 copying French plans, and now on display at Hartlepool.)*

(Above) Two relieved couples from the 68th Foot; the lottery to pick the six wives per company who could accompany the battalion overseas took place on the quayside, and was immediately followed by painful partings at short notice. The number of wives per battalion who sailed for the Peninsula varied between about 25 and 50, and there might be a couple of dozen small children as well. Careful unit records were kept, detailing names, ages and descriptions. Once in the field the army could do little for them, and there are many heartbreaking descriptions of widows and orphans falling behind during hard retreats like Corunna and Burgos. Few seem actually to have been killed, but many died of exhaustion, hunger, exposure or illness and those captured by the enemy were callously used.

(Left) A child of the camp. The five-year-old Elizabeth Gale, daughter of a soldier, helped her mother cut bandages at Waterloo, and saw many dead. She was still alive in Norwich in 1903, and may have been the last surviving British eyewitness.

There are dozens of examples in period memoirs of the women who followed the armies, and their characters and fates were as various. Some were sturdy and fearless, defying orders to the extent of risking the lash in their determination to provide their men with what small comforts they could at the end of the day's march. Some helped drag their sick or wounded husbands, and their muskets and packs, along the terrible roads during winter retreats. Some, piteously, took lanterns and searched the dreadful battlefields by night among the looters and cutthroats, frantic to find their men among the dead and dying – and occasionally found them in time, and nursed them back to health. Many never did find out what had become of their men, and were left to shift for themselves as best they could.

An epitome of the most formidable of these women is Bridget, broad-beamed wife of Dan Skiddy of the 34th Foot in the Peninsula. Stories of her and her donkey The Queen of Spain enliven the memoirs of Ensign Bell, but one instance must represent all. When the battalion was ordered to make an opposed assault crossing of the river Nive, and the women were strictly ordered to stay behind, Mrs Skiddy announced that she had the smallest donkey of them all, but that she would swim it across if she had to: "... But let me see who's to stop me, Bridget Skiddy, who travelled from Lisbon here into France. If Dan falls, whos to bury him? God save us! Divil a vulture will ever dig a claw into him while there's life in Biddy, his lawful wife. Now, girls, you may go or stay" – and with that she began to saddle her beast.

Some women, it must be admitted, were also shameless beggars, looters and riotous drunkards, whose behaviour goaded the military authorities to distraction. Besides the "official women", there were also crowds of determined Portuguese and Spanish followers of the oldest profession, such as have been attracted by all armies since the dawn of time; one French officer described their army in Spain as a mobile bordello. Wellington wrote that "It is well known that in all armies the women are at least as bad, if not worse, than the men as plunderers." He was always concerned about camp followers appropriating supplies: "The followers of the army, the Portuguese women in particular, must be prevented by the provosts from plundering the gardens and fields of vegetables...."

An earlier general order had also warned: "Officers commanding divisions and brigades, will be pleased to take measures to prevent the women, and followers of the army from buying up the bread which is prepared for the soldiers rations. This practice, carried on in the irregular manner it is at present, must ultimately prejudice the soldiers, and prevent the regular supply of bread." The women were also to be prevented from moving ahead of the army and purchasing bread in the villages, within two leagues of the station of any division of the army; when a woman required to buy bread she was to ask the officer of the company to which she belonged for a passport countersigned by the commanding officer of the regiment.

Wellington considered himself plagued by the numerous and undisciplined camp followers. In 1809 he issued the following: "The Commander of the forces observes that the women of the regiments have come up from Lisbon along with the clothing, to the great inconvenience of the army and to their own detriment: and as they travel on the carts,

Ladies visiting a British officer in camp, a popular adventure when on home service. Many officers' wives followed them to the Peninsula, some staying in Lisbon but others accompanying them on campaign and sharing all hardships and dangers. Many took young children with them, and some gave birth in grim conditions. Some were famous for their courage and kindness, like Mrs. Dalbiac of the 4th Dragoons, who rode with her husband the colonel at the head of the column with a small haversack and water bottle on her saddle, and slept with him under the open sky. The "delicate" Susanna Dalbiac searched for his body on the ghastly field of Salamanca, quite alone and by night, after Le Marchant's charge; he had in fact survived, and next day she was, as always, busy tending the wounded. The beautiful and fearless Lady Waldegrave of the 15th Dragoons – "I have seen her for four days together amongst the skirmishers" – once escaped capture by a French patrol by pressing her pocket pistol against a French trooper's chest. Some, however, like the vulgar, drunken and foul-mouthed Mrs. Morris of the 18th Light Dragoons, were a trial to all around them (though her husband was reportedly just as bad).

(Left) French generals confident of victory were sometimes tempted to take their mistresses with them on campaign – an arrangement that naturally became known to the humblest private in their army within days, if not hours. If the general won his battles the soldiers tended to regard his charming companion as a sort of mascot: Napoleon's mistress in Egypt, Pauline Fourès, was nicknamed Cleopatra and Our Lady of the East. On the other hand, when Marshal Masséna was forced to lead his starving army on the wretched retreat out of Portugal in March 1811, it is said that his mood was not improved by the constant nagging of one Mme Leberton – once such a delightful companion, in her fetching costume of dragoon green …

(Below) When a soldier's wife or a capable and cheerful camp woman was left widowed by the fortunes of war she had no lack of suitors, and it was not unusual for her to marry again fairly briskly – sometimes three or four times in succession, if she was persistently unlucky. Sometimes it was the only way to keep her place on the official ration strength; sometimes it was simply the realistic acceptance that a woman in her situation, however strong, was safer with a recognised protector.

Resourceful and uncomplaining, as ingenious at foraging as their men, and usually ready to help the chronically overworked surgeons tend the wounded after a battle, the women who accompanied the armies often earned a grudging respect even from the officers whom they so exasperated by clogging up the roads followed by the column of march. Landmann of the Royal Engineers recalled overtaking a lone Englishwoman striding along with a parasol, a straw bonnet and a large basket while he was riding along a Portuguese road strewn with corpses and under occasional cannon fire. When he suggested that she seek a place of safety "…she drew herself up, and with a very haughty air and, seemingly, a perfect contempt of the danger of the situation … she replied 'Mind your own affairs, sir. I have a husband before me.' I obeyed."

they delay and render uncertain, the arrival of the regimental clothing for the troops, and defeat all arrangements for bringing it up to the army. The Commander of the forces desires that Colonel Peacocke will prevent the women from leaving Lisbon with the clothing and regimental baggage; and the officers and non-commissioned officers coming up from Lisbon, in charge of clothing, are desired to prevent the women from travelling on the carts." One can all too easily imagine the scenes which must have arisen from attempts to enforce that particular order: a bashful teenage ensign, come out to join the army for the first time, trying to turn off a wagon the likes of Bridget Skiddy ... .

Senior officers almost invariably saw women as a nuisance. Under *The Rules and Regulations for the Cavalry* officers were to explain to the men that their womenfolk on campaign would be exposed to "many miseries". The more progressive Sir John Moore, in his *System of Training*, looked at the problem from the other direction: "The marriage of soldiers is a matter of benefit to a regiment, a comfort to themselves, or of misery to both, exactly in proportion as it is under good or bad regulations."

(Above) Junior officers such as Kincaid of the Rifles found the camp women useful, since when they were not present "The ceremony of washing a shirt amounted to a servant taking it by the collar and giving it a couple of shakes in the water and then hanging it up to dry." Even when the British army reached France in 1814, the French girls were no more cold to an English officer's charm than were their parents to the extraordinary British army habit of paying for provisions rather than pillaging.

"Mademoiselle was really an exceedingly nice girl, and the most lively companion in arms (in a waltz) that I ever met."

In the French army it was not unknown for *vivandières to reveal themselves as tender-hearted, in which case they were termed grivoise ("saucy"). However, French camp women who committed some serious offence might be sentenced to be "waxed" – stripped, shaved, and covered in boot blacking before being paraded around the camp.*

MARCHING, ALWAYS BLOODY MARCHING

The strength of an army, like the power in mechanics, is estimated by multiplying the mass by the rapidity; a rapid march augments the morale of an army, and increases all the chances of victory.

(The Emperor Napoleon)

The fires are lighted, camp kettles begin to boil; night falls and everyone has done his best to improvise some sort of shelter - but an aide-de-camp, a real kill-joy, arrives at the gallop, and soon an order, passed along our line, stops our preparations. We must move out without drum beat or trumpet call; to camp again 1,000 paces further on. We leave our campfires burning and will light our new ones at our new campsite. The enemy will believe that there are 20,000 men in the area, though there really are only 10,000. This manoeuvre is doubtless very clever, but the 10,000 do not appreciate it. (Elzéar Blaze)

T he campaigning season opened in the spring as orders covering the thousand details of moving an army and its impedimenta were written, and copies despatched to the dispersed winter encampments via the aides-de-camp. If an order miscarried or the message-rider was killed on the road then a whole brigade or division might fail to move, with potentially disastrous consequences. It was usual for important orders to be sent by more than one messenger, often taking different routes.

Once the orders reached the formations the clock was ticking. Every man, beast, piece of equipment and type of supply had to be inspected and if necessary replaced, repaired or replenished. Camps had to be struck and everything packed on wagons and mules. Herds of bullocks to provide fresh meat had to be gathered and controlled. The schedules for the order of march had to be studied, and the hundred different elements of the army had to be assembled on the right day, on the right road and in the right order – and all this by word-of-mouth and hand-written, hand-carried messages.   At last, on the appointed day, the march began. The leading cavalry clattered out first, then the parties who would plan and mark the first nights camps, and finally the slow, ever-stretching and contracting columns of tens of thousands of infantry, marching to their appointed destinies.

Barrès of the French Imperial Guard ironically described joining his new company: "Each of us was issued fifty cartridges, four days' rations, and accompanying utensils. I had the very great advantage of being the first selected to carry the cooking pot of my squad, as the most junior in service."

Of course, what seemed a good idea to an army commander did not always appear so good to those attempting to carry out his order. As Blaze put it, "We marched to the right, to the left, forward, sometimes backwards; in short we were always marching: very often we knew not why." The lack of roads meant that divisions ordered to follow different routes nevertheless sometimes crossed one another's path, causing delay and confusion, especially when these unhappy meetings involved the great supply trains of horse and ox wagons and herds of ration beef on the hoof.

A young Frenchman marching out on his first campaign recorded in his diary for 31 August 1805: "We left Paris quite

A stretch of early 19th century road surface near Waterloo. This stone metalling represents the best sort of main road used by Napoleonic armies; the paving usually extended only a short distance outside most towns, and most cross-country routes were of unsurfaced dirt even in relatively prosperous regions. In undeveloped countries such as Spain, Poland, the Ukraine and Russia paved roads were virtually unknown.

content to go campaigning rather than march to Boulogne. I was especially so, for war was the one thing I wanted. I was young, full of health and courage, and I thought one could wish for nothing better ... I was broken to marching; everything conspired to make me regard a campaign as a pleasant excursion on which, even if one lost ones head, arms, or legs, one should at least find some diversion. I wanted, too, to see the country, the siege of a fortress, a battlefield. I reasoned, in those days, like a child.

"And at the moment of writing this, the boredom which is consuming me in cantonments (at Schönbrunn) and four months of marching about, months of fatigue and wretchedness, have proved to me that nothing is more hideous, more miserable, than war."

Blaze believed that "No man ever knew how to make an army march better than Napoleon. These marches were frequently very fatiguing; sometimes half the soldiers were left

Generals might regard horses as expendable equipment, and their riders were necessarily unsentimental, but there were limits to their detachment. Many were horrified when, at the end of the British retreat to Corunna, the cavalry horses could not be taken aboard the ships and were ordered to be destroyed. "The beach was covered with dead horses, and resounded with the reports of the pistols that were carrying this havoc amongst them. The animals ... appeared frantic, neighed and screamed in the most frightful manner." Another witness wrote: "Many of the cavalry officers ... could not bring themselves to kill the horses which had been their companions - aye, and even their means of salvation ... and they allowed them to run free ... One of these poor brutes followed the boat which bore its master – an officer of the 18th Hussars – to the transport, and twice swam like a dog from the shore to the ship ... All those who witnessed this incident had tears in their eyes."

behind; but as they never lacked goodwill, they did arrive, though they arrived later."

The speed of march varied greatly, depending upon the terrain, the weather and the circumstances. In the Peninsula the redcoats reckoned to cover an average 15 miles (24km) a day. In the blazing summer they rose not long after midnight and marched in the cool darkness, halting again between mid-morning and mid-afternoon, and sometimes put some more miles behind them in the evening. With hourly halts of ten minutes, they could keep this up for weeks at a time, covering many hundreds of miles with very few complete days of rest. In an emergency they could cover the ground much faster; famously, in July 1809 the British light infantry and riflemen of Craufurd's Light Brigade force-marched 66 miles (106km) from Coria to Talavera in 30 hours.

From a French soldier in Spain we read that: "The forced marches of our army often continued until late at night, and in passing the squadrons we frequently heard Italians, Germans or Frenchmen singing their national airs to lull their fatigue or ... to recall a lively remembrance of their distant homeland. The army stopped very late at night near deserted towns or villages, and on our arrival we generally found ourselves in absolute want of everything; but the soldiers soon dispersed on all sides to forage, and in less than an hour they collected at the bivouac all that yet remained in the neighbouring villages."

Forced marches were one of Napoleon's secret weapons. He would divide his forces, show weakness to the enemy, invite him to attack – and lo and behold, on the day of battle the Emperor would magically produce enough troops to make his opponent believe himself outnumbered three to one. General Savary was congratulated by Tsar Alexander three days after the victory at Austerlitz. It seemed obvious to Alexander that the French were everywhere numerically superior to the

(Above) British officer dressed for the march, with an oilcloth cover laced over his bicorn hat and a plain over-coat. Senior officers got first pick of any buildings for shelter or had their own tents; but most junior officers shared the luck of their men, sleeping in the open under makeshift shelters of branches, bracken and horse blankets. The experienced used their small allowance of baggage transport for a voluminous boatcloak or other water-proof garment, a tarred cloth bag for stuffing with straw or ferns to make a paliasse, blankets, a pillow and a leather nightcap.

Military camps on the line of march were not always scenes of rain-lashed misery, however; when troops occasionally got a chance to rest in one place for a while in good weather bivouac life was pleasant enough. Off duty, smoking, drinking, gambling and women were the soldiers main diver-sions (not necessarily in that order). The British often played football, cricket, fives, and other games. Bell of the 34th entered a recently abandoned French long term camp on the Nivelle, where comfortable huts "had their green blinds over their little lattice windows; their neat little fireplaces, bedsteads of green boughs, shelves for

their prog (food), and arm-racks ...."

Mercer described an overnight Prussian bivouac in 1815 as "... a more cheering scene. There all was life and movement. Their handsome horses, standing harnessed and tied to the car-riages, sent forth neighing ... Dark forms moved amongst them; and by the bivouac fires sat figures that would have furnished studies for a Salvator. Dark, brown, stern visages, rendered still stern-er by the long drooping moustache that overshadowed the mouth, from which appended their constant companion, the pipe." German troops were famous in the Peninsula for their wonderful singing on the march and in camp.

(Opposite) These two French light cav-alry officers are having a friendly practice bout; duels were, however, a frequent occurrence, though very rarely pursued to the death. The practice was called "refreshing oneself with the sabre", and first blood usually settled the matter. Even at the Fontainebleau military school "... they fought with bayonets, but a student having been killed, the school suppressed that weapon. That didn't stop the duelling; we acquired foils, bit by bit, and in a pinch we used compasses attached to the end of a stick – all to give ourselves a dashing air."

Austrians and Russians. Savary replied: "What really happened was that we moved about a good deal and that individual divisions fought successive actions in different parts of the field. This is what multiplied our forces throughout the day, and this is what the art of war is all about. This was Napoleon's fortieth battle, and he never goes wrong on that point."

A famous forced march by French cavalry was that of 1806, during the pursuit of the Prussians after Jena, when Lasalle's 5th and 7th Hussars spearheaded the most decisive pursuit ever conducted by a pre-mechanised force. They covered the following distances:

14-20 October: Jena, Erfurt, Langensalfza, Nordhausen, Halberstadt, Magdeburg – 125 miles (200km) in six days.
21-28 October: Dessau, Spandau, Prenzlau – 168 miles (270km) in eight days. Hohenlohe surrenders.
29 October-7 November: Stettin, Friedland and Anklam, Schwerin, Lübeck, Ratkau – 200 miles (320km) in ten days. Blücher surrenders.

The total distance covered was thus approximately 500 miles (800km) in 24 days; some stages covered 40 or 50 miles in 24 hours.

The weather and landscape naturally had a major effect on both the speed of march and the morale of the troops. Napoleonic armies marched through every kind of conditions, from near-desert in Spain to the icy horrors of the Russian winter, and from mountain passes to fever-ridden wetlands, by way of everything in between.

The agonies of the retreat from Moscow are too well recorded to need examples here. After covering a few exhaust-ing miles through the snow each day the starving soldiers crowded into any kind of shelter for the night; their fires sometimes got out of control and burned hovels and men together. When they could find no buildings they lay huddled together in the snow around campfires, wrapped in layers of anything they could find – sacking, gun tarpaulins, scraps of looted carpet – and when they staggered on each morning some of their comrades were left behind, stark and frozen where they lay.

In summer the heat in Spain was murderous; the metal of weapons, buckles, even stirrup irons became too hot to touch. Men died of heat exhaustion under their 60lb (27kg) loads, caked with abrasive dust from head to foot, their faces bloody from inflamed sores; some held leaves in their mouths to shade their sun-swollen and cracking lips.

All soldiers probably hate mud worse than any other conditions, and dirt roads churned by the passage of armies in rainy weather became deep quagmires. Wagons and guns bogged down, had wheels wrenched off and overturned; men slipped and fell at every step; horses lurched and stumbled as they dragged themselves along in knee-deep clay. Colonel Vivian wrote from south-west France in winter 1813: "For ten days I have been covered with mud. You can have no conception of the sort of lanes – I can't call them roads – that we have here; up and down stiff hills, knee deep in mud. From head to foot we are all covered."

The contrasts could be startling; Blakeney of the 28th Foot wrote of the fighting in the Pyrenees: "Dripping with perspiration from hard fighting and scorching rain in the val-

(Left) A French hussar patrol scouts forward during the 1813-14 campaigns. On the march in potentially hostile country the cavalry recconoitred well ahead of the slow bulk of the army, provided a rearguard, and threw out flank screens to prevent surprise attacks on the columns. They got the first pick of any loot; but equally, their horses' constant need for forage meant that they were forced to range further and further away from the mass of the army as it ate its way across country, and such parties were often ambushed. Foraging parties carried reaping hooks and scythes, and stuffed their harvest into large nets slung from the saddle. Horses are notoriously delicate in respect of their diet, and huge numbers became sick on campaign through the lack of proper feed.

(Right) A trooper of the French 5th Hussars rides easy, with a cigar clamped in his mouth. Smoking was popular in all Napoleonic armies; although most soldiers used pipes, the armies which had campaigned in the Peninsula picked up the local taste for cigars, which in Spain were smoked by both sexes and all ages down to quite young children. Elzéar Blaze recalled that even at his military school at Fontainebleau the pupils smoked in the latrine: "Some thirty intrepid smokers would brave the effluvium which the tobacco smoke could not always neutralise. Had they been condemned to smoke there, they would have screamed to high heaven, but it was forbidden, therefore it was delightful. It appears that, for certain men, to smoke is a thing of absolute necessity, like bread or like air. One day I overheard several officers talking about the various privations that they had experienced before, during and after the battle of Eylau; one complained of not having any bread for three days, another of having to eat horse meat, a third of having had nothing to eat at all. Then an old hussar officer said, with the greatest composure, 'And there was I, who during five days was obliged to smoke hay'."

leys, we had immediately to clamber up to the top of high mountains and face the extreme cold naturally to be found there and dense fogs, which soaked through us and are more penetrating and oppressive than heavy rain."

Elzéar Blaze wrote of the relative advantages enjoyed by the French Imperial Guard on the march, "whose sufferings were not to be compared with those of the Line. The Imperial Guard ... (was) composed of picked men, who could easily have carried a heavier knapsack. It always marched on the high road, with the headquarters; it monopolised all the attention of the administration, and it may be asserted that the Line got no supplies until the Imperial Guard was served.

"Our conscripts were bent under the weight of a knapsack, a musket, a cartouche box; add to these fifty ball cartridges, bread, meat, a kettle, or perhaps a hatchet, and you may form some conception of the plight of those poor fellows, especially in hot weather. The perspiration trickled from their brows; and in general, after marching for three successive days, they were obliged to go into the hospital. Our marches were far more toilsome than those of the Imperial Guard; we had to travel along much worse roads; and I think I am warranted in asserting that fatigue killed more young conscripts than the cannon of the enemy."

Even a brief stop while on the march, to answer a call of nature or adjust ones kit, could present problems: "We found it difficult to march on account of the mud, which was sticky and tenacious on this black, heavy soil. Already I was finding it difficult to drag my feet out of it when I had the misfortune of discovering that one of my trouser straps was broken. As it

was impossible to go on walking, I stopped to put on another, but in the meantime the infantry were arriving, with the cavalry and the artillery of the Guard (my battalion formed part of the vanguard). I was forced to wait until all this mass of troops had gone by, in order not to be crushed, jostled, lost in this host, itself lost in the mud ... This took a long time, there being so many troops. At last I threw myself headlong into a squad of our own men."

For the sick, lame and shirkers, dropping out of the line of march while travelling through fat, smiling countryside might be attractive. It was a good deal less so when campaigning in enemy country in one of Europe's grimmer wildernesses. In Russia the fate of stragglers caught by the lurking Cossacks, or by vengeful peasants, was likely to be harsh; at the hands of the swarming guerrillas in Spain it was often too dreadful to describe. In both theatres of war wolves were still plentiful and fearless, and for the straggler or the abandoned wounded they added an extra horror to the prospect of death from simple starvation and exposure.

Albert de Rocca of the 2nd Hussars gave colourful details of a French bivouac in the Peninsula: "Around large fires, lighted at intervals, all the implements of military cooking were seen. Here they were busy constructing in haste cabins of planks covered with leaves for want of straw; there they were erecting tents, by stretching across four stakes such pieces of stuff as had been found in the deserted houses. The ground was strewn up and down with the skins of the sheep just slain, guitars, pitchers, bladders of wine, the cowls of monks, clothes of every form and colour; here the cavalry

under arms were sleeping by the side of their horses, further on a few of the infantry, dressed in women's clothes, were dancing grotesquely among the piles of arms to the sound of discordant music."

When on the march an army could be "like wolves driven into the open by hunger." Although forbidden to enter "a rather pretty village", a group of Frenchmen disobeyed the order and entered anyway. "I was in a courtyard with a number of other Chasseurs in the act of cutting up a pig we had just killed, when Marshal Lefèvre, Commander of the Foot Guard, entered with General Rousset, Chief of Staff of the Imperial Guard. We were frozen with terror ... At first they were very angry and threatened to have us shot; but having heard us they said, half in anger, half laughing, 'Get off to the camp, sharp, you confounded brigands; take your spoil, but so no one sees it, and above all don't get caught by the patrols'." On another day, or caught by another senior officer, the affair could easily have ended very differently; French discipline in the matter of looting could be confusingly arbitrary, since soldiers were often ordered to plunder the countryside. When they did so, it was not a matter of a few laughs over a liberated pig.

(Above) Most soldiers of all armies were issued low shoes, which were supposed to be held in place by the gaiter strap passing under the instep; but on rough ground this was quite inadequate. Shoes provided by rascally contractors often disintegrated after only a week of use; British army shoes were particularly bad. We often read of men on long marches reduced to wrapping their feet in rags; in the Peninsula soldiers made crude rawhide moccasins from the hides of ration bullocks, or acquired local hemp espadrilles.

(Far left) Well-equipped French soldier of the Fusilier-Grenadiers of the Young Guard. The Guard were issued special high quality greatcoats, and prided themselves on their appearance even in the field. As a Grenadier he carries a sabre as well as a bayonet. Strapped to his cowhide knapsack are spare shoes – riches indeed; his clay pipe is stuck in his oilcloth-covered shako; his tobacco pouch, and perhaps his purse, may be inside it.

(Left) Men of the 127th Line from Hamburg take a short pause during a summer march; note their cloth shako covers and thin campaign trousers. In all armies such items as trousers wore out quickly after a few months of marching and sleeping in the open; they were often replaced using any available local cloth, and regiments soon acquired a multi-coloured appearance.

(Right) Some French soldiers were issued with tinned iron water canteens, but these rusted quickly. Most acquired their own, and bottles with wicker covers were popular. So, for their strength and lightness, were dried natural gourds, which were cultivated to grow in a convenient shape with a swollen neck to take a stopper and a slinging cord.

Since the dawn of history a ravaging army has been, with good reason, the peasant farmer's worst nightmare. Armies took not just the crop in the fields, but the food stored to feed the village through the winter, and the seed corn for next year's planting; not just this year's beasts, but the cow saved from the salting-trough to provide the next generation. They took the family's only plough horse or mule, their tools, their fences and doors for firewood. In the wake of a marauding army whole communities were doomed to beggary or even starvation in the long term – and in the short term, when the next hungry regiment arrived and demanded what had already been stolen, they might face torture and atrocious murder.

★ ★ ★

Understandably, much is made of Napoleon's armies living off the land; but under most circumstances his staffs made huge efforts to provide rations for his men (it was he, after all, who said that an army marches on its stomach). Often, however, they failed miserably, causing hardship for his hungry soldiers, and ruin for the inhabitants of the lands over which they passed like locusts. In 1805 the Grande Armée were ordered from the Channel coast camps where they had sat staring at

England, and marched east to fight another enemy. The Boulogne camps had not included the full logistic train which was considered, until then, necessary to sustain large European armies in the field. Transportation for supplying 170,000 men was thus required in a few short weeks. The intended recipients of these supplies were already marching towards the Rhine, along with 80,000 new recruits en route to their units. This was all orchestrated by Napoleon's chief-of-staff Marshal Berthier, who wrote: "It is the Emperor's intention ... to feed the troops en route as they were fed in the camps."

Orders had gone ahead to local authorities to provide supplies for the advancing host, with rations issued every two or three days. The marshals were also to use their initiative and live off what the country might supply. Bernadotte's corps took seven days' biscuit ration with them so as not to ravage neutral Hesse-Kassel; in the early days the Emperor was more thoughtful towards his allies than he became later.

The horses suffered worse than the men. Thick mud, rain and insufficient fodder took a heavy toll on the animals. When the corps were in position on the Rhine, Marshal Soult possessed only 700 of the 1,200 horses necessary to draw his sup-

ply train. As usual the uncomplaining beasts were the worst-treated members of the army, a short-sighted policy which left the later Empire bereft of suitable livestock.

The plans involved setting up advance supply depots along the route, Napoleon ordering 500,000 biscuit rations split evenly between Wurzburg and Ulm. This and other suitable measures were to keep the army supplied until it reached Bavaria, although they put a massive strain on available resources and it was hardly surprising that the effort was to partially fail. Similarly the necessary transport was also lacking, not enough time being allowed for its collection. What Napoleon demanded and what he received differed considerably. When the French army halted its advance, as at Ulm in 1805, local sources of supply would soon become strained; however, such pauses did allow a regular supply link to be established with the rear areas.

Soldiers' rations were supposed to be 1½lb of bread, ½lb of meat, 1oz of rice or 2oz of dried fruit per day. On campaign this was to be provided by the population upon whom the soldiers were forcibly quartered. (Officers, of course, ate at their hosts' table and expected considerably more.) Receipts were to be given for amounts received, and good luck to those who presented them ...

Once in the enemy's territory his own military depots and magazines could be overrun, and his towns terrorised into providing supplies to the invaders. This was sufficient for the leading elements of a corps, but later arrivals were often not so fortunate. In general enough supplies were carried or appropriated to keep the army moving until in close proximity to the enemy, when it often became necessary for regiments to look after themselves. The cavalry, of course, were ideally placed for this task, and they mounted excursions to seize any likely village before the infantry could arrive; by the time they did there was little left for the footsloggers.

When fighting in fertile regions – the Low Countries, northern Italy, Austria, Bavaria – as long as an army continued to win and to advance, it was able to sustain itself by taking what it needed from the population. In poor or unevenly developed countries – Spain, eastern Poland and the Ukraine, above all in Russia – this so-called system broke down completely, with disastrous consequences for all. Napoleon summed up the dilemma most succinctly when speaking of Spain, where "small armies are beaten, and large armies starve."

For the Russian invasion of 1812 the Emperor was faced with supplying his largest ever army in a comparative wasteland. He increased the train service to 26 battalions, eight of which were equipped with 600 light and medium vehicles, the others with 252 four-horse wagons with a capacity of 1.5 tonnes; and 6,000 reserve horses were to keep the supplies moving. Heavy wagons were chosen to minimise horse numbers, since they gave a better horse-to-load ratio than lighter ones. The more horses used, of course, the more fodder required to feed them, requiring even more transport to carry the fodder .... In the event the horses starved and froze to death. At least their emaciated cadavers provided some food for the human survivors straggling back towards Poland.

★ ★ ★

Once forced into retreat an army could soon turn into a dwindling column of pitiful refugees. In winter 1808 an unbeaten British army were forced by the collapse of their Spanish allies to retreat across the Galician mountains towards a rendezvous with the Royal Navy at the port of Corunna:

"Each seemed to look upon his neighbour as an abridgement to his own comforts. His looks seemed to say, one or other of the articles you wear would be of great use to me; your shoes are better than those I possess; if you were dead, they would be mine... .

"The officers, in many points, suffered as much as the men. I have seen officers of the Guards, and others, worth thousands, with pieces of old blankets wrapped round their feet and legs; the men pointing at them, with a malicious satisfaction, saying 'There goes three thousand a year' ...

"I came up with a cluster of poor devils who were still alive, but apparently, both men and women, unable to proceed. They were sitting huddled together in the road, their heads dropping forward, and apparently patiently awaiting their end. Soon after passing these unfortunates, I overtook a party who were being urged forward under charge of an officer of the 42nd Highlanders ... pretty much as a drover would keep together a tired flock of sheep ... Many of them had thrown away their weapons, and were linked together arm in arm in order to support each other, like a party of drunkards ... Many were bare-headed, and without shoes; and some with their heads tied up in old rags and fragments of handkerchiefs."

Commissary Schaumann of the KGL wrote: "The enemy did not need to inquire the way we had gone; our remains marked out his route ... Starving inhabitants of the country fled in front and past us with faces distorted by fear, despair and vindictiveness; and the weaker among them ... laden with their belongings and perishing from the fear, and from the rain, the storms, the snow and the hunger ... sank in the mire at our feet, imploring in vain for help, which we could not

(Above) The redcoats' most basic and all too frequent overnight accomodation. Where possible troops naturally camped in the edge of woodland, for shelter and fuel, but in many parts of Europe woodlands capable of sustaining tens of thousands of men had been cleared centuries before 1800. Some men spread their single blanket on a mat of foliage; reversed the greatcoat and stuck their legs into the sleeves, pulling the buttoned skirts up round them like bedclothes; arranged the knapsack for a pillow; pulled their forage cap down around their ears; and hoped for the best. The blue object is the heavy wooden "Italian" water canteen; this was sometimes proofed inside with beeswax, incidentally giving the water a honey taste.

give our own men.

"The road was strewn with dead horses, bloodstained snow, broken carts, scrapped ammunition boxes, cases, spiked guns, dead mules, donkeys and dogs, starved and frozen soldiers, women and children ... I saw one bullock cart belonging to the paymaster general's department loaded with six barrels full of Spanish dollars ... A soldier with bayonet fixed stood guard over the treasure, and with a desperate air implored every officer that passed by to relieve him of his duty ... nobody paid any heed; the most confirmed thief passed by unmoved.

"Further on a Portuguese bullock driver lay dead beside his fallen bullocks, a soldier's wife had taken shelter beneath his cart, but she too was lying lifeless; and the tragic part of it was that her child ... was whimpering and trying to find nourishment at her frozen breasts. One or two officers had the child taken from her, and wrapping it in a blanket, carried it away."

RATIONS

Most armies attempted to issue quite generous quantities of basic rations in the field; their variable success depended upon the region and season, and the practicalities of transport and distribution. Food was issued collectively to squads, and the men usually cooked and ate their rations together. The staple was bread, when bakeries could be set up near enough for the wagons to reach the army in reasonable time; or when they could not then sometimes flour, which the soldiers mixed with water and salt into unleavened cakes for baking in their campfire embers, or dumplings for their stewpots.

In the British army the daily bread ration was 1½lbs, but when it failed to arrive (or was too mouldy even for ravenous soldiers) then each man was to receive 1lb of hard ship's biscuit. Charles Napier wrote in 1811: "We are on biscuits full of maggots, and though not a bad soldier, hang me if I can relish maggots." Rice was occasionally issued instead; and sometimes oatmeal, which the soldiers brewed into a gruel they called "stirabout."

Ration beef was sometimes salted, which took too much time and water to soak properly; but it was usually fresh, butchered on the spot each night from the herd accompanying the column (with about 45,000-50,000 men Wellington's Peninsula army used some 300 head a day). It was tough and stringy, and took a lot of cooking. Usually the impatient men fried it, or broiled it on their ramrods; if they had the time they boiled it into a stew or soup with anything else that was available from local foraging or purchase. As throughout history, any chickens or pigs in the vicinity of the army which did not have the protection of an armed guard were usually doomed.

Fruit, vegetables and pulses were sometimes plentiful; but on other occasions the men had to make do for days at a time by filling their pockets with large acorns. If the British army was famished then it was usually, by definition, marching in country from which the civilians had fled; at such times the strict prohibition on looting was relaxed, and anything edible was gathered from the deserted fields. In friendly country the locals brought in food for sale, including dairy products.

(Oddly, William Surtees, then of the 56th Foot, tells us that while serving in Ireland in 1800 "Potatoes were out of the question, for they were no less than three shillings a stone of fourteen pounds"; and that subsequently there were "innumerable robberies of potato fields; and many were the men punished for this crime.")

Like Jack Tar, the redcoat was also entitled to a daily ration of alcohol – a third of a pint of rum or a pint of wine; local brandy or gin was sometimes substituted. If he had liquor and tobacco then he could usually forget his troubles for a while. Officers drew rations like their men, but were obviously better placed to buy extra food locally when it was available, and goats were sometimes kept for milk. Leslie of the 29th Foot: "Our standard dishes for dinner were a certain portion of ration beef made into soup, with rice, turnips, onions, carrots and tomatoes. These being long stewed, the soup was nutritious and the beef was always tender. Another portion of our ration beef was made into steaks, fried with onions … "

★ ★ ★

Mercer, after the battle of Waterloo: "I now began to feel somewhat the effects of my long fast … . My joy then may be imagined when, returning to our bivouac, I found our people returned from Linois, and better still, that they had brought with them a quarter of veal, which they had found in a muddy ditch, of course, in appearance then filthy enough. What was this to a parcel of men who had scarcely eaten a morsel for three days? In a trice it was cut up, the mud having been scraped off with a sabre, a fire kindled and fed with lance-shafts and musket-stocks; and old Quartermaster Hall, undertaking the cooking, proceeded to fry the dirty lumps in the lid of a camp kettle. How we enjoyed the savoury smell! And having made ourselves seats of cuirasses, piled upon each other, we soon had that most agreeable of animal gratifications – the filling of our empty stomachs. Never was a meal more perfectly military, nor more perfectly enjoyed."

★ ★ ★

French soldiers took it in turns to cook the squad rations, which were supposed to be bought locally with unit funds set aside for the purpose from their pay. An order of 1809 specifies for the Grenadiers of the Guard a ½lb of trimmed meat daily, 28oz of bread (including some white bread for crumbling into their soupe, the usual soldier's habit), 2oz of dried vegetables, salt, and half a pint of wine. Troops billeted at Stralsund in 1812 had a daily ration of 1½lbs of ammunition bread (two parts rye to one part wheat flour), 4oz of wheat bread for the soup, 10oz untrimmed meat, 8oz of dried vegetables or 2lbs of potatoes, salt, and one-sixteenth of a pint of brandy.

At most times and places on campaign they ate, in practice, what they happened to receive or could find, steal or extort, boiled up in the camp kettle: any kind of cattle, game or fowl, with rice, potatoes, and/or any other available vegetables. When there was no salt they used gunpowder. At the start of the Russian campaign fresh bread was plentiful; the units would send flour wagons and rustled cattle ahead on their line of march to search out houses with ovens and cook the meal ready for their arrival. Water became scarce and of bad quality as they marched east; by Borodino some units were having to dig six or eight feet down to find dirty yellowish water which had to be filtered (if there was time, through a barrel filled with layers of clean straw, gravel and charcoal). The loot in Moscow included not only grain, peas, nuts, etc., but also fine wines and delicacies like sugar, coffee and chocolate. Even at the start of the retreat there was no bread except for the "doughboys" or galettes cooked in the ashes; anyone who wanted to eat had to take his turn making them. By the end of the campaign a man had to buy his place under shelter or beside a fire with a contribution of some sort of food. Before the Berezina crossings a Polish officer reported being offered a stew made of human flesh by Croatian troops.

★ ★ ★

The French musician Girault, on the island of Lobau during the 1809 Aspern-Essling campaign: "I found a flask of grease … there had been many geese plucked and cleaned the night before by the first-comers, but I found some discarded livers and hearts … one of my comrades had found some flour, and we made a galette in the embers. And on a later occasion: "I had half a biscuit left, which I shared with my comrade … I went for a look around, and found some soldiers cutting up a splendid cuirassier's horse. I joined in, and as I had a good knife I was able to take away a good cut off the thigh … My comrades would have taken it for beef if I had stopped to skin it first … We made a fire, and at the end of two hours ate it half-cooked and without salt. It was not good… but hunger overcame my disgust."

CHAPTER 8
FIELDS OF GLORY

The first consideration with a general who offers battle should be the glory and honour of his arms; the safety and preservation of his men is only the second. (The Emperor Napoleon)

When a young soldier saw his first action he was unlikely to forget it: "A little farther on, however, we met a Russian yager, or rifleman, coming back and holding out his hand, which had been wounded, and from which the blood was flowing pretty copiously. This was the first blood that I had ever seen as drawn in hostile conflict, and it certainly produced a somewhat strange effect upon me; it showed plainly that we were in the immediate vicinity of that enemy we had so often talked about, and whom we hoped to conquer; that now the time had arrived which would infallibly prove what every man, boaster or not, was made of; and that it might happen that it was my lot to fall."

Others were affected slightly differently: "This was the first blood I had ever seen shed in battle; the first time the cannon had roared in my hearing, charged with death. I was not yet seventeen years of age, and had not been six months from home. My limbs bending under me with fatigue, in a sultry clime, the musket and accoutrements that I was forced to carry were insupportably oppressive. Still I bore all with invincible patience. During the action the thought of death never once crossed my mind. After the firing commenced, a sensation stole over my whole frame, a firm determined torpor, bordering on insensibility. I heard an old soldier answer, to a youth like myself who inquired what he should do during the battle, 'Do your duty!'"

One young Frenchman thought that "The din of the artillery breaching the defences of Ulm was so loud and so terrible, one might have thought the whole world was being destroyed." At night whilst looking for firewood a French soldier "loaded a dead Austrian on my shoulders, having taken him for a log. This startled me terribly."

Cornet Tomkinson of the 16th Light Dragoons was almost killed very early on in his career: "We galloped about one hundred yards down the road, then turned into the enclosures to the right, through a gateway in a stone wall sufficiently wide for one horse. I was nearly off, my horse turned so suddenly. On getting into the enclosure, we rode at a gallop up to the enemy, who strange to state, ran away. They were scattered all over the field, and I was in the act of firing my pistol at the head of a French infantryman when my arm dropped, without any power on my part to raise it. The next thing I recollect was my horse galloping in an ungovernable manner amongst this body of infantry, with both my hands hanging down, though I do not recollect being shot in the left arm. In this state one of their bayonets was stuck into him, and he fortunately turned short round; and I had, in addition, the good luck to keep my seat on him."

Eventually Tomkinson knocked his head on a low branch, and regained consciousness being supported by a French infantry soldier who took him to a shaded wall. "In

a short time some of the German infantry came up (belonging to our advance under General Paget), and began to plunder me, taking out of my pocket a knife containing many useful things for campaigning. They were prevented proceeding any further by the arrival of Private Green, who took me for Captain Swetenham, telling me I was certainly killed and that it was a sad thing to order men on such a duty."

Eight men had accompanied Tomkinson into the field; Green was the only one to escape, one man being shot in nine places. Green was made up to sergeant; Tomkinson lived through his ordeal, being "wounded by a musket shot in the neck. It had entered above the left shoulder and come out in the front. A second through the right arm, above the elbow, and a third musket shot through the left, below the elbow, with a bayonet wound close by the latter. The wounds were dressed in the common and best manner, being bound up in their own blood."

★ ★ ★

Storming a fortified town was one of the deadliest tasks for infantry; when the artillery blew a `practicable breach' in the walls the enemy usually had plenty of time to barricade it against the storming parties. They would use wooden beams chained together, thickly set with old sword blades and spikes to make a *chevaux de frise*; powder charges might be buried in the breach, and explosive and incendiary bombs prepared for hurling at the attackers. As they clawed their way up they faced point-blank musketry and cannon fire from defenders massed at the threatened point. William Laurence of the 40th Foot was one of the 'forlorn hope' in the assault on Badajoz in April 1812:

"We were supplied with ladders and grass bags, and ... at length the deadly signal was given, and we rushed on towards the breach. I was one of the ladder party ... On our arriving at the breach, the French sentry on the wall cried out 'Who comes there?' three times ... but on no answer being given, a shower of shot, canister and grape, together with fire-balls, was hurled at random amongst us. Poor Pig received his death wound immediately, and my other accomplice, Bowden, became missing, while I myself received two small slug shots in my left knee, and a musket shot in my side, which must have been mortal had it not been for my canteen: for the ball penetrated that and passed out, making two holes in it, then entered my side slightly.

"...We found a *chevaux de frise* had been fixed and a deep entrenchment made, from behind which the garrison opened a deadly fire on us. Vain attempts were made to remove this fearful obstacle, during which my left hand was dreadfully cut by one of the blades ... My wounds were still bleeding, and I began to feel very weak; my comrades persuaded me to go to the rear; but this proved a task of great

difficulty, for on arriving at the ladders, I found them filled with the dead and wounded, hanging some by their feet just as they had fallen and got fixed in the rounds. I hove down three lots of them, hearing the implorings of the wounded all the time; but on coming to the fourth, I found it completely smothered with dead bodies, so I had to draw myself up over them as best I could."

While Lawrence crawled away from the fighting to try to get his wounds dressed, at another part of the walls Joseph Donaldson of the 94th confronted a scene which, apart from the firearms, was essentially medieval:

"...The cannon and musketry which played upon our troops from every quarter of the town ... kept up a continual roll of thunder, and their incessant flash one quivering sheet of lightening; to add to the awfulness of the scene, a mine was sprung at the breach, which carried up, in its dreadful blaze, the mangled limbs and bodies of many of our comrades.

"When the ladders were placed, each eager to mount, crowded them in such a way that many of them broke, and the poor fellows who had nearly reached the top, were precipitated a height of thirty or forty feet, and were impaled on the bayonets of their comrades below; other ladders were pushed aside by the enemy on the walls, and fell with a crash on those in the ditch; while more who got to the top without accident were shot on reaching the parapet, and tumbling headlong, brought down those beneath them."

★ ★ ★

Emmanuel von Warney described a correct method of mounting a cavalry charge as the whole regiment moving forward at the first trumpet call, the first line supported by the second and the reserve. At the second (doubled) call, the whole begin to trot; the second line and reserve maintain the trot until the charge is completed. The third (tripled) call is given at 150 to 200 paces from the enemy. At this signal the first line canters; when within 70 or 80 yards of the target a fanfare of trumpets should signal the gallop, the soldiers raking back their spurs and pushing on their horses. At 20 paces the bridles are slackened, the spurs wilfully applied, and the full impulse of the charge is given. Upon impact the second line is to support the first, the reserve to complete a victory or cover a retreat. That was the theory; in practice one side usually broke before contact, or both sides would slow and the impact that was intended to overthrow the enemy would be dissipated, resulting in a swirling mêlée. Sometimes, however, a clash occurred such as this one at Waterloo:

"The French had barely time to wheel up to the left and push their horses into a gallop, when the two bodies came in collision. They were at a very short distance from us, so that we saw the charge perfectly. There was no check, no hesitation, on either side; both parties seemed to dash on in a most reckless manner, and we fully expected to have seen a horrid crash – no such thing! Each, as if by mutual consent, opened their files on coming near, and passed rapidly through each other, cutting and pointing, much in the same manner one might pass the fingers of the right hand through those of the left. We saw but few fall. The two corps reformed afterwards, and in a twinkling both disappeared, I know not how or where."

continued on page 130

Usually the last side that held a reserve carried the day. This was alluded to by Lord Uxbridge, commander of the British cavalry at Waterloo, when describing the aftermath of the wild pursuit by the heavy brigades after their repulse of d'Erlon's corps: "After the overthrow of the Cuirassiers I had in vain attempted to stop my people by sounding the rally, but neither voice nor trumpet availed; so I went back to seek the support of the 2nd Line, which unhappily had not followed the movements of the heavy cavalry. Had I, when I sounded the rally, found only four well formed squadrons coming steadily along at an easy trot, I feel certain that the loss the first line suffered would have been avoided, and most of these guns might have been secured."

The French light cavalry leader General Lasalle considered excess galloping to be fruitless. "Look at those mad sods", he would say while watching enemy cavalry; "Let them wear themselves out!" He would keep his own troops well in hand at a controlled trot; only when the enemy tired on their approach did he order the triple gallop which would usually decide the issue.

★ ★ ★

Infantry, when charged by cavalry, formed square to maximise the density of their all-round firepower and of the defensive ranks of bayonets, leaving no opening through which a horseman might charge. While these dense masses of human flesh and steel were, when formed by steady infantry, almost impervious to cavalry attack, they were extremely vulnerable to artillery and the sniping of skirmishers. It is instructive to read rather more of the Waterloo memoir of Ensign Leeke, 52nd Light Infantry, than we quote at the head of Chapter 5:

"I distinctly saw the French artilleryman go through the whole process of spunging out one of the guns and reload-

ing it; I could see that it was pointed at our square, and when it was discharged I caught sight of the ball, which appeared to be in a direct line for me. I thought, Shall I move? No! I gathered myself up, and stood firm, with the colour in my right hand. I do not exactly know the rapidity with which cannon-balls fly, but I think that two seconds elapsed from the time I saw this shot leave the gun until it struck the front face of the square. It did not strike the four men in rear of whom I was standing, but the four poor fellows on their right.

"It was fired at some elevation, and struck the front man about the knees, and coming to the ground under the feet of the rear man of the four, whom it most severely wounded, it rose, and passing within an inch or two of the colour poles, went over the rear face of the square without doing any further injury. The two men in the first and second ranks fell outward, I fear they did not survive long; the two others fell within the square. The rear man made a considerable outcry on being wounded, but on one of the officers saying kindly to him, `O man, don't make a noise', he instantly recollected himself and was quiet ... .

"It was said, after the action, that a round shot had expended its force on the solid square of the 71st Highland LI on our right front, and only stopped when it had killed or wounded seventeen men; I can easily suppose this to be possible from what I saw of the effects of the shot which passed so close to me."

Sergeant Morris of the 2/73rd Foot: "On (the cavalry's) next advance they brought some artillerymen, turned the cannon in our front upon us, and fired into us with grapeshot (canister), which proved very destructive, making complete lanes through us; and then the horsemen came to dash in at the openings. But before they reached, we had

closed our files, throwing the dead outside, and taking the wounded inside the square ... .

"We saw the match applied, and again it came as thick as hail upon us. On looking round, I saw my left hand man falling backwards, the blood falling from his left eye; my poor comrade on the right, also by the same discharge, got a ball through his right thigh, of which he died a few days afterwards."

Sergeant Lawrence of the 40th: "About four o'clock I was ordered to the colours ... There had been before me that day fourteen sergeants already killed and wounded while in charge of those colours, with officers in proportion, and the staff and colours were almost cut to pieces ... I had not been there more than a quarter of an hour when a cannon-shot came and took the captain's head clean off. This was again close to me, for my left side was touching the poor captain's right, and I was spattered all over with his blood."

Another witness wrote: "During the battle our squares were a shocking sight. Inside we were nearly suffocated by the smoke and smell from burnt cartridges. It was impossible to move a yard without treading upon a wounded comrade, or upon the bodies of the dead; and the loud groans of the wounded and dying were most appalling. At 4 o'clock our square was a perfect hospital, being full of dead, dying and mutilated soldiers.

"The charges of cavalry were in appearance very formidable, but in reality a great relief, as the artillery could no longer fire on us: the very earth shook under the enormous mass of men and horses. I never shall forget the strange noise our bullets made against the breastplates of Kellermann's and Milhaud's Cuirassiers, six or seven thousand in number, who attacked us with great fury. I can only compare it with a somewhat homely simile, to the noise of a violent hail storm

beating upon panes of glass.

"The artillery did great execution, but our musketry did not at first seem to kill many men: though it brought down a large number of horses, and created indescribable confusion. The horses of the first rank of Cuirassiers, in spite of all the efforts of their riders, came to a standstill, shaking and covered with foam, at about twenty yards distance from our squares, and generally resisted all attempts to force them to charge the line of serried steel. On one occasion, two gallant French officers forced their way into a gap, momentarily created by the discharge of artillery; one was killed by Colonel Staples, the other by Captain Adair. Nothing could be more gallant than the behaviour of those veterans, many of whom had distinguished themselves on half the battlefields of Europe."

Captain Gronow described the doomed splendour of the mass charge of the French cavalry at Waterloo. "About 4 p.m. the enemy's artillery in front of us ceased firing all of a sudden and we saw a large mass of cavalry advance: not a man present who survived could have forgotten in afterlife the awful grandeur of that charge. You perceived at a distance what appeared to be an overwhelming, long moving line, which, ever advancing, glittered like a storm wave of the sea when it catches the sunlight. On came the mounted host until they got near enough, whilst the very earth seemed to vibrate beneath their thundering tramp. One might suppose that nothing could have resisted the shock of this terrible moving mass. They were the famous Cuirassiers, almost all old soldiers who had distinguished themselves on most of the battlefields of Europe. In an almost incredibly short period they were within twenty yards of us, shouting *Vive l'Empereur!*

"The words of command 'Prepare to receive cavalry'

had been given, every man in the front ranks knelt, and a wall bristling with steel, held together by steady hands, presented itself to the infuriated cuirassiers ... The charge of the French cavalry was gallantly executed, but our well directed fire brought men and horses down, and ere long the utmost confusion arose in their ranks. The officers were exceedingly brave, and by their gestures and fearless bearing, did all in their power to encourage their men to form again and renew the attack ...

"Soon after the cuirassiers had retired, we observed to our right the red hussars (lancers) of the Garde Impériale charging a square of Brunswick riflemen, who were about fifty yards from us. This charge was brilliantly executed, but the well sustained fire from the square baffled the enemy, who were obliged to retire after suffering a severe loss in killed and wounded. The ground was completely covered with those brave men, who lay in various positions, mutilated in every conceivable way. Among the fallen we perceived the gallant colonel of the hussars, lying under his horse, which had been killed. All of a sudden two riflemen of the Brunswickers left their battalion, and after taking from their helpless victim his purse, watch and other articles of value, they deliberately put the colonel's pistols to the poor fellow's head and blew out his brains. 'Shame! Shame!' was heard from our ranks, and a feeling of indignation ran through the whole line: but the deed was done: this brave soldier lay a lifeless corpse in sight of his cruel foes, whose only excuse perhaps was that their Sovereign, the Duke of Brunswick, had been killed two days before by the French." (Gronow

was mistaken; the officer was not the commander of the Red Lancers – General Colbert survived.)

"The enemy cavalry had to advance over ground which was so heavy that they could not reach us except at a trot; they therefore came upon us in a much more compact mass than they probably would have done if the ground had been more favourable. When they got within ten or fifteen yards they discharged their carbines to the cry of *Vive l'Empereur!*, but their fire produced little effect, as is generally the case with the fire of cavalry. Our men had orders not to fire unless they could do so on a near mass; the object being to economise our ammunition, and not to waste it on scattered soldiers. The result was that when the cavalry had discharged their carbines and were still far off, we occasionally stood face to face, looking at each other inactively, not knowing what the next move might be."

★ ★ ★

Even in the midst of battle soldiers could still laugh. Three British officers came to watch the effect of the cannonade, one of them carrying an umbrella. When French roundshot started arriving in the British ranks the officers moved off back towards their own corps "... although only a few yards in the rear, scampered off in double quick, doctor and all, he still carrying his umbrella aloft. Scarcely though had he made two paces when a shot, as he thought, passing rather too close, down he dropped on his hands and knees – or I should rather say hand and knees, for one was employed in holding the silken cover most pertinaciously over him – and away he scrambled like a great baboon, his head turned fear-

fully over his shoulder, as if watching the coming shot, whilst our fellows made the field resound with their shouts and laughter."

★ ★ ★

Cavalié Mercer of the British RHA described how "suddenly a dark mass of cavalry appeared for an instant on the main ridge and then came sweeping down the slope in swarms, reminding me of an enormous surf bursting over the prostrate hull of a stranded vessel, and then running, hissing and foaming up the beach. The hollow space became in a twinkling covered with horsemen, crossing, turning and riding about in all directions, apparently without any object. Sometimes they came pretty near us, then would retire a little. There were lancers amongst them, hussars and dragoons – it was a complete mêlée. On the main ridge no squares were to be seen; the only objects were a few guns standing in a confused manner, with muzzles in the air and not one artilleryman. (Wellington had ordered that they shelter in the infantry squares when the charges reached them.)

Sir Augustus Frazer, in charge of artillery, came up to Mercer: "I rode with Frazer, whose face was as black as a chimney-sweep's from the smoke, and the jacket sleeve of his right arm torn open by a musket ball or case-shot, which had merely grazed his flesh." Frazer was repositioning Mercer's battery "about one third of the distance between Hougoumont and the Charleroi road", and informed him that "in all probability we should immediately be charged on gaining our position.... The Dukes order's however are positive. In the event of their (the French cavalry) persevering

and charging home, you do not expose your men, but retire with them into the adjacent squares of infantry."

Mercer then describes how, as they approached the reverse slope, "We breathed a new atmosphere – the air was suffocatingly hot, resembling that issuing from an oven. We were enveloped in thick smoke, and despite the incessant roar of cannon and musketry, I could distinctly hear around us a mysterious humming noise ... cannon shot too ploughed the ground in all directions, and so thick was the hail of balls and bullets that it seemed dangerous to extend an arm lest it should be torn off."

The battery took up their position between two Brunswick infantry squares: "The Brunswickers were falling fast – the shot every moment making great gaps in their squares, which the officers and sergeants were actively employed in filling up by pushing their men together and sometimes thumping them ere they could make them move." Upon deploying, the horse artillerymen soon had a column of French cavalry approaching at a trot, "not more than one hundred yards distant, if so much, for I do not think we could have seen so far. I immediately ordered the line to be formed for action – case shot! And the leading gun was unlimbered and commenced firing almost as soon as the word was given: for activity and intelligence our men were unrivalled.

"The very first round, I saw, brought down several men and horses ... the carnage was frightful ... Every discharge was followed by the fall of numbers, whilst the survivors struggled with each other, and I actually saw them using the

pommels of their swords to fight their way out of the mêlée. Some, rendered desperate at finding themselves thus pent up at the muzzles of our guns, as it were, and others carried away by their horses, maddened with wounds, dashed through our intervals – few thinking of using their swords, but pushing furiously onward, intent only on saving themselves."

A French account of the same action gives the view facing Mercer's guns from the other side of the hill. "Through the smoke I saw the English gunners abandon their pieces, all but six guns stationed under the road, and almost immediately our cuirassiers were upon the squares, whose fire was drawn in zigzags. Now I thought, those gunners would be cut to pieces; but no, the devils kept firing with grape, which mowed them down like grass."

The dangers of being a gunner were not limited to the enemy's fire and steel. "Gunner Butterworth was one of the greatest pickles in the troop, but at the same time, a most daring, active soldier; he was No.7 (the man who sponged etc.) at his gun. He had just finished ramming down the shot and was stepping back outside the wheel, when his foot stuck in the miry soil, pulling him forward at the moment the gun was fired. As a man naturally does when falling, he threw out both his arms before him, and they were blown off at the elbows. He raised himself a little on his two stumps and looked up most piteously in my face." Butterworth was sent to the rear; his body was found next day lying by the roadside where he had bled to death.

The French cavalry sniped at Mercer's battery: "One fellow certainly made me flinch, but it was a miss; so I shook my finger at him, and called him coqin, etc. The rogue grinned as he reloaded, and again took aim. I certainly felt rather foolish at that moment, but was ashamed, after such bravado, to let him see it, and therefore continued my promenade. As if to prolong my torment, he was a terrible time about it. To me it seemed an age. Whenever I turned, the muzzle of his infernal carbine still followed me. At length bang it went, and whiz came the ball close to the back of my neck, and at the same instant down dropped the leading driver of one of my guns (Miller), into whose forehead the cursed missile had penetrated."

As the charges continued, "Every man stood steadily at his post, the guns ready, loaded with a round-shot first and a case over it; the tubes were in the vents; the port-fires glared and sputtered behind the wheels; and my word alone was wanting to hurl destruction on that goodly show of gallant men and noble horses ...

"The column was led on this time by an officer in a rich uniform, his breast covered with decorations, whose earnest gesticulations were strangely contrasted with the solemn demeanour of those to whom they were addressed. I thus allowed them to advance unmolested until the head of the column might have been about fifty or sixty yards from us, and then gave the word, 'Fire!' The effect was terrible. Nearly the whole leading rank fell at once; and the round-shot, penetrating the column carried confusion throughout its extent. The ground already encumbered with the victims of the first struggle, became now almost impassable. Still, however, these devoted warriors struggled on, intent only on reaching us. The thing was impossible."

General de Brack, then a young officer in the Red Lancers, tells us that guns should be charged in skirmishing order to minimise casualties. "This method is good on perfectly level ground and when the guns are in a risky posi-

tion. But what the regulations do not tell us is that even on level ground you must, before charging the guns, have the ground reconnoitred by a few bold and well mounted skirmishers, who must not be too numerous, and who are too far from each other to fear the enemy firing at them. Without observing this precaution you run the risk of being stopped short before attaining your object, and returning with no other result than losses. General (Edouard) Colbert, at Wagram, took this precaution when the Emperor commanded him to charge the centre, and it was that alone which, preserving his brigade from useless loss, enabled him to employ it an hour later in assisting so brilliantly at the victory.

"One more precaution to be observed, if the guns which you are to charge are supported by infantry, is to direct your charge in such a manner as to keep the guns between this infantry and yourself; the fear of killing their gunners will prevent the infantry firing. The best way of capturing guns, especially on undulating country, is to threaten them with a false attack with half your troops, and to cut them off with the other half."

★ ★ ★

Sergeant Wheeler of the 51st Light Infantry, fighting on the right flank of the Allied army at Waterloo, saw the fate of one squadron of cuirassiers: "In one of these charges ... a great many overcharged themselves and could not get back without exposing themselves to the deadly fire of the infantry. Not choosing to return by the way they came they took a circuitous route and came down the road on our left. There were nearly one hundred of them, all Cuirassiers. Down they rode full gallop, the trees thrown across the bridge on our left stopped them. We saw them coming and

was prepared, we opened our fire, the work was done in an instant. By the time we had loaded and the smoke had cleared away, one and only one individual was seen running over the brow in our front. One other was saved by Capt.Jno.Ross from being put to death by some of the Brunswickers" (this was the 'noble fellow' who was seen by another witness turning back to rescue a dismounted comrade.)

"I went to see what effect our fire had had, and never before beheld such a sight in so short a space, as about an hundred men and horses could be huddled together where they lay. Those who were shot dead were fortunate, for the wounded horses in their struggles by plunging and kicking so finished what we had begun."

★ ★ ★

During the Peninsula War the French repeatedly came up against Wellington's reserve slope defence. The future Marshal Bugeaud, victor in Algeria in the 1840s, was a young soldier in the Peninsula, and leaves us the classic French infantryman's view:

"The English generally occupied well chosen defensive positions having a certain command, and they showed only a portion of their forces. The usual artillery action first took place. Soon, in great haste, without studying the position, without taking time to examine whether there were means to make a flank attack, we marched straight on, taking the bull by the horns. About 1,000 yards from the English line the men became excited, called out to one another, and hastened their march; the column began to become a little confused. The English remained quite silent with ordered arms, and from their steadiness appeared to be a long red wall. This continued on page 140

steadiness invariably produced an effect on our young soldiers.

"Very soon we got nearer, crying *Vive l'Empereur! En avant! À la baionnette!* Shakos were raised on the muzzles of muskets, the column began to double, the ranks got into confusion, the agitation produced a tumult; shots were fired as we advanced. The English line remained silent, still and immovable with ordered arms, even when we were only 300 yards distant, and it appeared to ignore the storm about to break. The contrast was striking; in our innermost thoughts we all felt the enemy was a long time in firing, and that this fire, reserved so long, would be very unpleasant when it came. Our ardour cooled. The moral power of steadiness, which nothing can shake (even if it be only appearance), over disorder which stupefies itself with noise, overcame our minds.

"At this moment of intense excitement the English wall shouldered arms; an indescribable feeling would root many of our men to the spot; they began to fire. The enemy's steady, concentrated volleys swept our ranks; decimated, we turned round seeking to recover our equilibrium; then three deafening cheers broke the silence of our opponents; at the third they were on us, pushing our disorganised flight."

★ ★ ★

Let the final words be of the true price of glory: the aftermath of a great battle. As Wellington said, "Next to a battle lost the greatest misery is a battle gained. Not only do you lose those dear friends with whom you have been living, but you are forced to leave the wounded behind you."

William Hay, a subaltern of the 12th Light Dragoons, passed over the field of Waterloo on 19 June, heading towards Brussels. "I was struck with horror at the actual masses of dead men and horses heaped together on a space of about a few hundred yards. The day was extremely hot, and the dead bodies, already offensive, were shocking to look at. Many wounded were among them, so disabled as

not to have the power to extricate themselves. On gaining the road it was with difficulty my horse could pick his way or keep his footing as it was literally paved with steel, the cuirasses were so numerous, shining and glittering in the midday sun of June, making it quite dazzling to the eyesight. The ditches on each side of the road were lined with our wounded officers and soldiers, who had been borne there to be removed in some measure from the great thoroughfare, amongst whom I recognised several acquaintances."

Those left on a Napoleonic battlefield too badly wounded to limp or crawl away by themselves simply lay where they had fallen until sheer luck decided their fate. Parties of troops from the victorious army were sent out to find the wounded and bury the dead, but this process could take days; great numbers of the badly injured died lingering deaths, and others were murdered by looters - soldiers and local civilians scavenging for coins, watches, or any other saleable plunder. Lieutenant-Colonel Frederick Ponsonby of the 12th Light Dragoons lay out all night on the field of Waterloo, cold and desperately thirsty; he had been wounded seven times, including a lance thrust which had collapsed a lung and left him with a sucking wound in his back. He had been roughly robbed by a French skirmisher; made as comfortable as possible and given a drink of brandy by a kindly French officer; and had later been ridden over by Prussian cavalry:

"I thought the night would never end. About this time I found a soldier lying across my legs, and his weight, his convulsive motions, his noises, and the air issuing from a wound in his side, distressed me greatly; the last circumstance most of all, as I had a wound of the same nature myself. ... The Prussians were wandering about to plunder: many of them stopped to look at me as they passed; at last one of them stopped to examine me: I told him that I was a British officer, and had already been plundered. He did not

however desist, and pulled me about roughly."

Ponsonby was exceptionally lucky: before midnight he attracted the attention of a straggler from the 40th Foot, who stood guard over him until next morning, when a messenger was sent to fetch a cart to carry him to Waterloo village and the attentions of his surgeon.

★   ★   ★

The aftermath of a Napoleonic battle often drew appalled but fascinated visitors. Miss Charlotte Eaton left this description of the field of Waterloo many days afterwards:

"On top of the ridge in front of the British position ... we traced a long line of tremendous graves, or rather pits, into which hundreds of dead had been thrown as they had fallen in their ranks. ... The effluvia which arose from them, even beneath the open canopy of heaven, was horrible; and the pure west wind of summer ... seemed pestiferous, so deadly was the smell that in many places pervaded the field. In many places the excavations made by the shells had thrown up the earth all around them ... The ground was ploughed up in several places with the charge of the cavalry and the whole field was literally covered with soldiers' caps, shoes, gloves, belts, and scabbards, broken feathers battered into the mud, remnants of tattered scarlet cloth, bits of fur and leather, black stocks and haversacs belonging to the French soldiers, buckles, packs of cards, books, and inumerable papers of every description ... printed French military returns, muster rolls, love-letters and washing bills; illegible songs, scattered sheets of military music, epistles without number ... literally whitened the face of the earth."

An anonymous gentleman tourist mentioned "vast numbers of cuirasses taken out of the water, into which they were thrown by the peasants for concealment, and afterwards sold for two francs each. Met waggons full of wounded, crying out from extreme suffering. The water everywhere quite red. ... All the wells at Waterloo spoiled by throwing men into them. Churches still full of wounded. ... We took a large quantity of camphor with us, as a preventetive against infection. Were much annoyed by the incalculable swarms of carrion flies ... Owing to the dry weather, the ground cracks and opens, and as the bodies of the men buried are not above a foot below the surface, they may still be seen in many places."

★   ★   ★

On the night of the 18th Mercer thought "It was a thrilling sensation thus to stand in the silent hour of the night and contemplate that field – all day long the theatre of noise and strife, now so calm and still – the actors prostrate on the bloody soil, their pale wan faces upturned to the moon's cold beams, which caps and breastplates and a thousand other things, reflected back in brilliant pencils of light from as many different points ...

"Horses too, there were to claim our pity – mild, patient, enduring. Some lay on the ground with their entrails hanging out, and yet they lived. These would occasionally attempt to rise but, like their human bedfellows, quickly falling back again, would lift their poor heads, and, turning a wistful gaze at their side, lie quietly down again, to repeat the same until strength no longer remained, and then, their eyes gently closing, one short convulsive struggle closed their sufferings. One poor animal excited painful interest – he had lost I believe both his hind legs; and there he sat the long night through on his tail, looking about, as if in expectation of coming aid, sending forth, from time to time, long and protracted melancholy neighing.

"Although I knew that killing him at once would be mercy, I could not muster courage even to give the order. Blood enough I had seen shed during the last six and thirty hours, and sickened at the thought of shedding more. There, then, he still sat when we left the ground, neighing after us, as if reproaching our desertion of him in the hour of need."

APPENDIX

Uniform facing colours for the British regiments in the Peninsula were as follows, based upon the 1802 Amended Descriptive View of the Clothing and Appointments of the Infantry. *Lace detail is mostly from Hamilton Smith's 1815 chart.*

LINE INFANTRY REGIMENTS

Regiment	Facings	Lace loop shape & spacing (s = single, p = in pairs)	Officer's lace & metal (G = gold, S = silver)
1st, The Royal	Blue	Square, p	G
2nd, Queens' Royal	Blue	Square, s	S
3rd, The Buffs, E.Kent	Buff	Square, p	S
4th, The King's Own	Blue	Square, s	S
5th, Northumberland	Gosling yellow	Square, s	S
6th, 1st Warwick	Deep yellow	Square, p	S
7th, Royal Fusiliers	Blue	Square, s	G
9th, E.Norfolk	Light yellow	Square, p	S
11th, N.Devon	Full green	Square, p	G
14th, Bedford	Buff	Square, p	S
29th, E.Devon	Pale yellow	Square, p	S
23rd, Royal Welsh Fusiliers	Blue	Square, s	G
24th, Warwick	Willow green	Square, p	S
26th, Cameronian	Pale yellow	Square, p	S
27th, Enniskillen	Buff	Square, s	G
28th, N.Gloster	Bright yellow	Square, p	S
29th, Worcester	Yellow	Square, p	S
30th, Cambridge	Pale yellow	Bastion, s	S
31st, Huntingdon	Buff	Square, s	S
32nd, Cornwall	White	Square, p	G
34th, Cumberland	Bright yellow	Square, p	S
36th, Hereford	Green	Square, p	G
38th, 1st Stafford	Yellow	Square, s	S
39th, E.Middlesex	Green	Square, p	S
40th, 2nd Somerset	Buff	Square, p	G
44th, E.Essex	Yellow	Square, s	S
45th, Nottingham	Deep green	Bastion, p	S
47th, Lancashire	White	Square, p	S
48th, Northampton	Buff	Square, p	G
50th, West Kent	Black	Square, p	G
57th, W.Middlesex	Yellow	Square, p	G
58th, Rutland	Black	Square, s	G
59th, 2nd Nottingham	White	Bastion, s	G
61st, S.Gloster	Buff	Square, s	S
62nd, Wiltshire	Yellowish buff	Square, p	S
66th, Berkshire	Yellowish green	Square, s	S
76th	Red	Square, p	S
77th, E.Middlesex	Yellow	Square, s	S
80th, Staffordshire Volunteers	Yellow	Square, p	G
81st	Buff	Square, p	S
82nd, Prince of Wales	Yellow	Bastion, p	S
83rd	Yellow	Square, p	G
84th, York and Lancaster	Yellow	Square, p	S
87th, Prince of Wales Own Irish	Green	Square, p	G
88th, Connaught Rangers	Pale yellow	Square, p	S
89th	Black	Square, p	G
90th, Perthshire Volunteers	Deep buff	Square, p	G
91st	Yellow	Square, p	S
94th	Green	Square, p	G
97th, Queen's Own	Blue	Square, p	S

LIGHT INFANTRY REGIMENTS

43rd, Monmouth	White	Square, p	S
51st, 2nd Yorkshire	Deep green	Square, p	G
52nd, Oxford	Buff	Square, p	S
53rd, Shropshire	Red	Square, p	G
68th, Durham	Deep green	Square, p	S
71st, Highland	Buff	Square, s	S
74th, Highland	Yellow	Square, s	G
85th, Buckingham	White	Square, p	S

LIGHT CAVALRY REGIMENTS

1803 (based upon the De Bosset Diagrams)

Regiment	Jacket	Facings	Lace
7th LD	Blue	White	S
8th LD	French grey	Scarlet	S
9th LD	Blue	Pale buff	S
10th LD	Blue	Yellow	S
11th LD	Blue	Pale buff	S
12th LD	Blue	Pale yellow	S
13th LD	Blue	Pale buff	G
14th LD	Blue	Orange	S
15th LD	Blue	Scarlet	S
16th LD	Blue	Scarlet	S
17th LD	Blue	White	S
18th LD	Blue	White	S
19th LD	French grey	Yellow	S
20th LD	Blue	Yellow	S
21st LD	Blue	Pale yellow	S
22nd LD	French grey	Scarlet	S
23rd LD	Blue	Yellow	S
24th LD	Blue	Yellow	S
25th LD	French grey	Red	S
26th LD	French grey	Red	S
27th LD	French grey	White	S
28th LD	French grey	Yellow	S
29th LD	Blue	Pale buff	S

Notes: *9th & 11th LD, buff breeches; 13th LD, pale buff breeches; 10th LD, a frame around the lace.*